Benita Galeana

BENITA

translated by
Amy Diane Prince

Latin American Literary Review Press
Pittsburgh, Pennsylvania
Series: Discoveries
1994

The Latin American Literary Review Press publishes Latin American creative writing under the series title *Discoveries*, and critical works under the series title *Explorations*.

This project is supported in part by grants from the National Endowment for the Arts in Washington, D.C., a federal agency, and the Commonwealth of Pennsylvania Council on the Arts.

Library of Congress Cataloging-in-Publication Data

Galeana, Benita.
    [Benita. English]
    Benita / by Benita Galeana ; translated from the Spanish by Amy Diane Prince.
      p. cm.
    ISBN 0-935480-69-2 (alk. paper) ; $15.95
    1. Galeana, Benita--Biography. 2. Authors, Mexican--20th century--Biography. 3. Communists--Mexico--Biography. I. Prince, Amy Diane. II. Title.
PQ7298.17A37Z46313   1994
972.08'2'092--dc20
[B]   94-26202
                                          CIP

Benita may be ordered directly from the Publisher:
                    Latin American Literary Review Press
                    121 Edgewood Avenue • Pittsburgh, PA 15218
                    Tel (412) 371-9023 • Fax (412) 371-9025

Cover photograph by Javier Aspe. Cover design by Lisa Pallo. Book design by Michelle Rozzi.

CONTENTS

FOREWORD
Ilan Stavans

The conversion of Frida Kahlo, since her death in 1954, into a mythical figure, surpassing even the stature of her abrasive husband Diego Rivera, carries a harmful, dangerous consequence: Mexican women today are appreciated through the distorted prism of her life and oeuvre. Octavio Paz once described Kahlo as "a fascinating artist and complicated figure, hunted by hostile phantoms." And Carlos Fuentes suggested that she reduced Hispanic culture to her own body, "so often sacrificed and denied." But one must go further: Kahlo made art of her suffering. She used images to attempt an expurgation of her own soul and, indirectly, that of her people. Blooded wounds, a divided identity, a paralyzed, contemplative self—Is Kahlo really an allegory of femininity south of the Rio Grande? Certainly not.

Paz himself has written outstanding pages in his 1950 classic *The Labyrinth of Solitude* about womanhood in Mexico. "The Mexican woman," he writes, "quite simply has no will of her own."

> Her body is asleep and only comes really alive when someone awakens her. She is an answer rather than a question, a vibrant and easily worked material that is shaped by the imagination and sensuality of the male. In other countries woman are active, attempting to attract men through the agility of their minds or the seductivity of their bodies, but the Mexican woman has a sort of hieratic calm, a tranquility made up of both hope and contempt. The man circles around her, courts her, sings her, sets his horse (or his imagination) to perform *caracoles* for her pleasure. Meanwhile she remains behind the veil of her modesty and immobility. She is an idol, and like all idols she is mistress of magnetic forces whose efficacy increases as their source of transmission becomes more and more passive and secretive.

Any tourist trip to Mexico City reveals Kahlo's noxious impact on everyday life. Her portraits are endlessly reproduced in newspapers, magazines, and textbooks. Scores of quarto volumes on her art, compiled by Hyden Herrera, Raquel Tibol, and other critics, are on display in supermarkets, fashionable stores, and even in restaurants. Photographs of Frida alone and alongside Diego, her father Guillermo Kahlo, and her lover Leon Trotsky, are available as postcards. Imitations of her idiosyncratic dresses and colorful hairbands, ubiquitously on sale, have become a corrosive fashion. The painter has no doubt traveled a long road from the role of passive wife of a notorious muralist to Mexico's equivalent of Marilyn Monroe: a scandalously baroque sex symbol—the embodiment of *la mujer mexicana*, a call for rebellion, a feminist new beginning.

And yet, as part of the Europeanized minorities who have ruled Mexico since colonial times, Frida Kahlo is pure fake: a hybrid, a consummate actress. She mastered the art of adapting native costumes to her labyrinthine personality, and then resold the package to her contemporaries and the world at large. Eternally divided between her native, maternal side, and her foreign, paternal ego, she was disliked by many while alive, and other enemies have emerged since she passed away. They accuse her of reinventing the ideal of the Mexican woman, turning it from a passive, secretive transmission into a full-blown artifice.

Kahlo's authentic, unimaginative double exists under the name of Benita Galeana, an outspoken activist also closely attached to Mexico's Communist Party. They share the year of birth: 1907 (although some claim that Galeana was three years younger). One was born in the nation's capital, the other in the state of Guerrero. As Galeana's fragmented memoirs, originally written in Spanish in 1940, reprinted time and again in Hispanic America, and hereby translated into English by Amy Diane Prince, testify, hers was a road painfully traveled. Benita transformed herself from an abused and seduced rural girl to a high-ranking freedom fighter, from anonymous sufferer to famous associate of José Clemente Orozco, José Revueltas, and Fidel Castro.

Aside from Kahlo, whom Galeana wholeheartedly detested, the neighboring nation south of the border has a shamefully short list of forthright, candid women, fictional and otherwise. The roster might include Hernán Cortés's mistress and translator La Malinche, the poet Sor Juana Inés de La Cruz, the wife of the corregidor of Querétaro, Josefa Ortíz de Domínguez, the Italian photographer Tina Modotti, Elena Poniatowska's well-known character Jesusa Palancares, and, of course, the ever-present Virgin of Guadalupe. Benita Galeana no doubt ranks high among them. Her autobiography is an invaluable document crucial to understanding ideological dissent in Mexico since the Partido Revolucionario Institucional came to power in 1929, a testament of the resistance and affirmation of Hispanic women throughout the twentieth century.

No human life is truly individual. Our acts are repetitious and fit within preconceived patterns. Galeana's odyssey is not unlike those of Danton and Robespierre, Rev. Martin Luther King Jr., David Ben Gurion, Lech Walesa and Rigoberta Menchú. Her chapters are marked by the sudden death of her mother, poverty, her father's alcoholism, syndicalism and the joining of forces with urban workers, persecution by the Pascual Ortiz Rubio and Abelardo Rodríguez regimes, imprisonment and torture. She was still a young girl when the lifeless body of José Guadalupe Posada was buried in a collective grave. At the time she learned about the revolts of Emiliano Zapata and Pancho Villa. Unfortunately, time has a way of ridiculing her past. As an adult Benita Galeana repeatedly made the wrong ideological allegiances: she befriended Orozco, she belittled Lázaro Cárdenas and then applauded his son Cuauhtémoc, she kissed her idol Fidel Castro in Havana, she even adored Panamá's General Manuel Antonio Noriega.

Alongside Pablo Neruda and many others, Benita Galeana was part of an ill-fated generation of Latin American left-wingers who saw hope in dogmatism and utopia in tyranny. She remained a devoted Marxist long after the fall of the Berlin Wall and the Balkanization of the U.S.S.R. But in spite of her stubbornness, in spite of her ideological and sexual temptations and her nearsightedness, Benita remains an attractive emblem due to her infinite courage. Indeed, her liaisons map an invaluable journey by women in Mexico from the periphery of culture and politics to centerstage.

It is no accident that the Taller de Gráfica Popular, Carlos Monsiváis, and cartoonist Abel Quezada pay tribute to her. Unlike the average Mexican female of her era, Benita's body was never asleep. She was not an answer rather than a question, and was never shaped by the imagination and sensuality of the country's male. Hers was not a hieratic calm, a tranquility made up of both hope and contempt. While she managed to outlive Frida Kahlo by over four decades Galeana's achievement was never histrionic. She might dress as an *acateca* or *tehuana*, but her costumes were never staged mannerisms.

Given our present-day insatiable thirst for exhibitionism, given the complexities of Mexico's collective identity, it is not at all surprising to me that Benita Galeana, and not Kahlo, remains a shadowy figure, a footnote in history.

Amherst, Massachusetts
June 1994

GET BENITA!
Introduction by Elena Poniatowska

There are women who take pride in having lived a full, fruitful life: children, an education, good taste, a comfortable home, abundant table, cordial conversation, open door to visitors. In 1989, we also have professionals in science and the humanities, in technology; women have made a name for themselves in public service. But none of them—and I would swear to this—has lived as hard, enjoyable, and magnificent a life as Benita Galeana; not one began as early, and no one has gone on as long. At eighty-six years of age, Benita Galeana is still fighting, walking tall (she wears a wooden corset) and will not leave the Party "until they send for me from the beyond."

"I am a Communist now and I will die a Communist, loving my Party."

"Ay, Benita, the Party always treated you so badly, men always treated you so badly, they didn't even teach you to read and write, you've suffered because of the Party . . . "

"I didn't suffer with Mario Gil, my husband, he never treated me badly. No, he was always more and more in love with me, he always looked out for me, any little thing I did, he encouraged me, he told me that I should speak in public and I don't think I'm a good speaker, or rather I'm always sticking my foot in my mouth. In thirty long years, I've never once been angry with him. The only time I got angry was when he died. Yes, at the hour of his death, then I did suffer . . . I feel in the bottom of my soul that he failed me by dying and he's failing me still."

"But that was Mario Gil, kindness himself, a generous man, a good soul, even if he was a Communist . . . "

"Also a great writer. Did you read *The Railroad Workers*? Did you read his column on the Nueva Rosita strike? He left me everything, everything I have, this house, these paintings, all the books, he left them all to me."

This was a few years ago at the house at 11 Zutano, Street, where Benita Galeana lived, in the second Colonia de Periodista, a winding, shady street that seemed to belong to her, because she walked it gracefully, she hosed it down, she planted flowers. Then, with a cigarette and a cup of coffee between her hands, she spoke of the Thirties, of the Forties, of the drivers, the messengers, the gossips, the poor people who stuck swastikas on their chests, because in the Forties wherever you looked you would see swastikas. That was when the Communist Party fought the hardest and when there was the most blood in the streets. "The students, the workers, men next to women, peasants and even soldiers would help us in the street fighting, because if you treat them well, soldiers can be very good people. It makes me mad when I hear people calling them assassins . . . In Mexico they really put their all in the fight against Fascism. And there were plenty of Mexican Fascists, Catholic Fascists, Fascist-Fascists, like Almazán who had it in his blood, and other underground Fascists."

In that interview so many years ago, Benita told me about her participation in the 1968 student movement.

"I took sandwiches to the students, I took them medicine, I told their parents when they were arrested, or where they were hiding. They would give me the names of people to ask after and I would tell the people outside, the ones they wouldn't let in: 'It's alright, they're still in there.' I was always allowed into Lecumberri Prison, the Black Palace we called it, and I would tell the ones inside about the others, the ones who couldn't get in to visit because those apes are always so nasty to the families—you know, the guards, the ones who escort you around.

But they already knew me. I went all the way in, all the way to the cellblocks and I would get information from everyone. The movement in '68 needed support from all the people, not just me; and people misunderstood; no, the workers were mad, they said the young people were just lazy, and why didn't they go back to their studies instead of starting riots. Later they started letting women into Lecumberri to see what had happened to their children. But at Tlatelolco, on October 2, the police beat them hard. I saw how they shot at them and then they were giving it to them in the head, and all over their bodies, they were so angry. Those students really pissed them off! That's why I made myself a messenger between the students and their parents.

Ten years earlier, I also helped the railroad workers, well, I helped them much more. There I was helping them protect their daily bread. I organized the women, the wives, the daughters, to see what we could do, well, I did what I could. They were assaulted in their homes, they dragged the children by their hair, and if they cried they'd drag them even harder and they beat them in anger. In Monterrey they destroyed the workers' movement—they also beat the women there. There were women living in train cars, and they went in and pulled them out and emptied the whole car, everything strewn all over the tracks, it was a terrible thing, with children crying. They went for the railroad men to put them in jail and since Gómez Z. and his men had decided to betray the cause, well everything was in place, and they sure gave enough money to the workers so they'd break the strike and work as scabs. But that movement was beautiful, I liked it better than '68.

Women fighters? Oh, I remember when López Mateos was President there was a very brave woman, a beautiful one, she wore *rebozos* and had long hair, she wore it in curls, very beautiful, very brave, Macrina Rabadán. I think she was married to one of the Arenales, I don't remember which one, maybe it was Polo, well anyway I really respected her and then she ran for deputy of the PPS[1] and she lost, so she ran in Guerrero and she lost and she ran again and lost again. She came over one day and told me about it.

'Look, Benita,' she said, 'I won. Look, it's all here, look at the ballots, look at all the proof but they're crooks; they say they've won and it's fraud.' Then I said to her as a joke: 'Why did you go to the PPS? Don't the PRI[2] have a machine for turning out deputies and senators?'

And she's off, she believes me, and there she goes, off to join the PRI, and there she was with Ramírez y Ramírez and Rodolfo Dorantes and Rafael Carrilo and others, all of them with the PRI, all with the PRI when earlier they had been with us. As quick as a wink, they go join the PRI. And then yes, Macrina became a deputy and it was all hugging and triumph with López Paseos. But since she was really on the left, at least in her heart, she made some very beautiful decisions, some wonderful speeches, she spoke beautifully so that everyone would understand her, and she defended the workers from Poza Rica. I think she was against La Quina, and then when she started talking for real they wanted to get rid of her. 'Nobody will get me down off this stage," she would say, "only when I'm dead. I am in the struggle with the workers, and if I step down it will be to go to the prisons and I will continue defending the people from there.' Hooray, hooray, and hurrah, and applause, applause, bam, bam, bam, feet stamping on the floor, boom, boom, in the Chamber of Deputies. Really she was a great deputy, she was a deputy who gave it her all for the people. But it didn't last very long because when women are given power, the delegates don't let them do anything. They want them just to say yes to everything. She wanted to fight, but they told her, the bosses, I think the big boss was Manuel Moreno Sánchez, the one from the Senate. 'Now, let's stop this,' he said to her. 'You're here to earn your salary and for your sweets and nothing more.'

From then on, it made Macrina truly sad, well always, I always saw her sad after that, not elegant like she used to be. She was like me, I've never liked being stepped on; they kept her down so she wouldn't get out of line.

But as for me, I was born out of line."

Juan de la Cabada and Pepe Revueltas talked about her constantly and Benita became a mythical personality.

Benita and Mario Gil had their house at number 10 Antonio Caso Street. One morning Polo Arenal went by to ask them to rent him a room. The house was very big and had many rooms, and he offered them ten *pesos* as rent. In those days, ten *pesos* was an exorbitant sum. The rent for the entire house was fifteen *pesos*, so Benita came out ahead. She immediately agreed.

She never saw her tenant. Benita would leave the house early to go to her cell meeting and she never saw Leopoldo come home. At night, when she returned, she didn't even see lights in his room. After a while she began to receive telegrams while Arenal was away: "Deliver to David." Since she couldn't read, she took them to the Party. No one there could figure them out because they were always in Russian or Chinese or Tzotzil.

The Party couldn't decode the messages at all. "There's no David living in my house," she would say. "Who's David?" The day after the last cable arrived, there was an item in the newspaper. "Trotsky's house robbed."

"Who's he?" Benita asked.

Benita, who had been in jail fifty-eight times, knew how to get around the police. She knew all their tricks, but one time, when they showed up at the house on Antonio Caso Street, they took her by surprise. "Whatever else happens, the police always find me."

"What do you want?" she asked them.

"We're looking for some dangerous killers, Communists. We're going to search the house from top to bottom. Out of the way."

"And your search warrant?"

They didn't have one.

"Well you'd better go get it, because no one gets in here without a warrant, not even if he's sent by God Himself."

Neither Benita nor her husband Mario Gil let the cops in. But they themselves went down to search the rooms that Leopoldo Arenal was staying in and to their surprise they found weapons, uniforms, and false moustaches.

Mario and Benita disassembled the weapons and carried them out in peices, every day, in their market bag. They tore up the uniforms and Benita put on the moustaches, because just like Frida Kahlo (whom she can't stand), Benita Galeana had hair on her upper lip; that is, both are women with moustaches, bushy eyebrows, and hair on their chests.

"I didn't like that tiresome old Frida at all, not at all, I just didn't like her. I couldn't stand her, because she was conceited, she was two-faced, she put on airs. I could wear Tehuana dresses, too; of course, not as beautiful or as jewelled as Frida's. Everyone loved to give her things, not only Diego, but others, many others, she had a fistful of admirers. Both men and women. We would see her at the demonstrations, but she was always with the artists; she never stood with us, the soldiers on the front line, not even by mistake. Now Tina Modotti, the photographer, she did join us. But not Frida, as much as she tried to make people believe otherwise. So much for that, why should people say things that aren't true. I really wanted to tell her a thing or two and she really wanted to talk with Benita."

Actually, Benita considered Frida Kahlo a bourgeois, rich, privileged and conceited, "with all her jewels." Just like Lupe Marín: "They never came near us. They were high class. The Communist Party was angry with Frida and Diego because they were inconsistent. The truth was, Diego and Frida were Trotskyites. They say that the old man, that Russian with his scruffy little beard, was crazy about her."

Among the artists who were involved: Juan de la Cabada, David Alfaro Siqueiros, Leopoldo Mendez, Jose Alvarado, the

Cuban Juan Marinello, German Lizt Arzubide, Teresita Proenza, Diego Rivera's secretary, and Elena Vazquez Gomez, her sister, Mirta Aguirre; Benita Galeana especially remembers the little boy José Revueltas.

One afternoon, Benita was hurrying through Red Square (Plaza Santo Domingo, called Red Square for all the blood that ran through it), going to her cell, a nervous boy of about fourteen pulled at her stockings. "I want to join the Communist Party," he told her.

"You? But you're just a kid; you're even too young for the Communist Youth." He insisted, and ended up crying. He had been thrown out of his house and had nowhere to go.

Benita took him home with her and gave him dinner. She put him up for a few days, they turned into weeks and those into months, and all those days, the boy would go on and on about the Party, until finally one night when Benita was preparing some ink bombs to throw at the American Embassy, she said to the boy: "Today might be your day; come with us."

She gave a bomb to little José outside the embassy. "Aim and throw." she said. José Revueltas threw it right on target and they took off running, with the police behind. Once they were far away, Benita caught her breath.

"José," she said, "you now belong to the Communist Youth."

Years later, Pepe Revueltas, now secretary of the Communist Youth, busy in his work, ignored Benita at a meeting. There she was with her rebozo over her shoulders, her braids and her cigarette, standing right in front of him, talking and talking, and he wasn't responding at all. He didn't pay the least bit of attention to her. Benita, her voice hoarse from speaking at so many meetings, was proposing a strike at the Zocalo to prevent the German army, who was visiting Mexico at the time, from marching there. It was in 1937 or who knows what year but some time around then.

Jose called on his comrades for order and didn't even turn his head around to look at Benita, things had to be done one by one; Benita insisted again, they started arguing and Jose called her an anarchist. "Oh, so I'm an anarchist, eh?" And pow! she lets loose with a punch. Because Benita was politically aware and she knew that anarchist and stinker were the same thing.

They started fighting and fighting until Benita was good and mad.

Later, at a meeting, they asked a furious Benita who had won.

"I did, of course," she said. "I knocked him down and then I punched him good."

The Benita of today is still tall, standing straight, very straight. The years haven't shrunken her as often happens with age. Her hair, now going from gray to white, has the same quality as when she was young, when she had thick, curly fuzzy black braids that made more than one head turn. Benita now wears long dresses, but when she was young she wore black skirts, tapered blouses, tailored suits, high heels, even dresses from Paris, the kind you see in the shop windows. She was always very well-dressed, very coquettish, so that the patron Paquito Iturbe wanted to give her a house and meanwhile he would invite her to dinner at Ambassadeurs, a really swank restaurant. Or he would take her to an all-night place, because Benita always went at night. The one they went to was the rewrite room for the Mexican reporters; it was where they wrote their articles and Rodrigo de Llano, an old white nasty-looking man, put the newspaper together at the bar, there with Dalmau Costa, the owner of the joint. Benita was very happy. he still has her coquettish habit of taking off her glasses when she goes out to parties.

She is very independent, very sure of herself, very certain in her decisions even though she can not read or write. She had a daughter with Salvador Solano, who later abandoned her, and how lucky, thank God, because he was just a disturbance. Her daughter died when she was twenty-four, from a bad heart. Mario Gil and Benita decided to adopt six girls, but even today she doesn't like them to be around her to protect or to take care of her. Everything she needs she can do for herself. She goes out in the morning to buy a chicken and cooks it herself. She lives on her memories. The 1985 earthquake, while she was living on #11 Zutano Street, in Colonia del Periodista, gave her a bad scare. She gathered her daughters around. "Okay, girls," she told them, "open the closet, take everything out, we're going to find someone who needs all this."

That day she gave away not only all her household goods, but also decided to give away her collection of books and paintings. Now, at eighty-six, she lives alone. Benita wants her daughters to be free, and above all, she wants to depend on no one. Her ulcer doesn't bother her a bit. She is a strong woman. "In 1985 I realized how many things I had that I didn't need," she says.

Two years later, a group of Cuban women invited her to Havana. Benita tells the story: "When I arrived at Havana I didn't feel anything. I had great illusions, I had dreamed of going to Havana and when we landed I didn't feel a thing, not emotion, not nervousness, not happiness, nothing.

The day of the meeting, I introduced myself to all the women there. Fidel Castro was five hours late. I was bored and hot, and I went to take a walk in the hallway. The comrades from Mexico started chanting: "Make Fidel let Benita into his office!"

A Cuban woman said she would check to see if the Comandante could meet with Benita. She came back and said very shamefully that he was busy and perhaps another day. Benita felt her dream had been shattered and she walked off.

Soon, the same Cuban woman ran over, all upset, to say that the Comandante was waiting for Benita to go in right now. Benita smoothed out her braids and walked over to the Comandante's office. She went in. And yes, now she started to feel like she was really in Cuba. The Comandante gave her a hug. "Did you really know Julio Antonio Mella?" he asked her.

"Of course. I helped protect his ashes in Mexico."

"Give me a hug!"

Benita seconded him: "And give me one!"

They embraced. "Can I ask you a favor, Commandante?" she said.

"Of course, what is it?"

"Can I give you a kiss?"

"Come give a kiss."

"Come give a kiss."

And Benita gave him a very loud kiss.

She went back to Mexico feeling satisfied. For her, visiting Cuba meant seeing Fidel. The rest was icing.

Years after Mella's death, Benita tells how a group of Communists, among them Juan Marinello, who was babbling away, were in the cemetery, trying to get Mella's ashes to send them to Cuba and the army wouldn't let them, because the Communists had no right to anything, not even a dead man's ashes. But finally the ashes were rescued and are now in Havana. Benita was able to see the statue of Mella that stands in front of the University of Havana.

Of course, Benita's personality is very energetic; she expresses her strength; she teaches us. To live a life like Benita's is a lesson in mental health and when you close *Benita*, you have to say, "What a tremendous human being!"

Today in Mexico, thanks to our own Virgin of Guadalupe, there are many strong women. Rosario Ibarra de Piedra, of course, is the one who has the most influence with the politicians. Even Manuel Clouthier respected her and loved her. Benita follows the tradition of Maria Pistolas, who told Carranza off for being a usurper. She could be the modern Adelita. She has something of Mariano Azuela's strongest female character, La Pintada, in *The Underdogs*, and she has much of Jesusa Palancares in *Hasta no verte Jesus mio*.

It is surprising to think that the uppity little girl who cut off two fingers of her brother-in-law's hand, the girl who was dying to own a pair of shoes, that this little girl from the state of Guerrero, is now the Benita who travels and answers the calling of journalists from all over Latin America. They still call for her as they called for her all during her life, through struggles, riots, in her fifty-eight jailings and her many pitched battles: "Get Benita."

Mexico City

[1] Partido Popular Socialista

[2] Partido Revolucionario Institucional, the governing party in Mexico since the Revolution.

Childhood

MY FATHER

I was two years old when my mother died. My father was a very rich man, he owned a lot of land. He started drinking when my mother died. He was a good man. I heard he used to fill his saddlebags with money and ride through the countryside giving coins to the poor. I don't know how he lost his money, but by the time I reached the age of reason, my father was poor, and spent all his time getting drunk in the *cantinas*.

My brothers and sisters and I were still young when my mother died, so we went to live with my sister Camila, the oldest in the family. My father loved us very much, especially me, but he was almost always gone, travelling from town to town and spending whatever money he had left.

He liked to play with us when he came to the house. He used to cry when I told him how my sister would hit me, and make me work hard.

"If only your mother were alive!" he'd say to me.

I remember one day he was lying in the hammock. My brother Agustín and I climbed up to play with him. He had one of us on each side. We were very happy, playing, but I was jealous of Agustín. I didn't like it that my father was paying more attention to him. So when he wasn't looking, I pushed my brother and knocked him off the hammock. "Get lost, bastard!" I said to him. My father got mad. "You're going to get a beating for that," he said. "Not for pushing your brother, but for saying 'bastard.' I don't want you talking like that."

He always carried a riding whip in his hand and I thought he was going to whip me with it. But then he pulled a rope loose from the hammock, folded it in two, and hit me with that. I cried a lot, mostly because it was the first time he had ever hit me.

He had always been rich, so he didn't know how to work. When he saw me chopping wood, he took the axe from me so he could help, but he couldn't do it; it flew off to one side. That's when I realized he didn't know how to do anything, and that was why, when he became poor, he couldn't keep his children from suffering.

My father hated Camila, his oldest daughter, because she treated us badly and also because she was so rude to him. Camila had seen the richer times and she wasn't used to being poor. She fought a lot with my father, and because he hated her, he never gave an inch.

"Listen, girl," Camila said to me one day, "your father sold a cartload of rice and went off to drink in the *cantina*. We have to be sure he uses the money to buy food, so go find him and get his money pouch."

I went to the cantina to spy on him. I saw him take out a handkerchief with money in it. He untied it. He took out some coins. He tied it up again and set the pouch on the ground, below the hammock. Then I crept in, took the pouch and ran home. But a friend of my father's saw me. "Your daughter just ran off with your money," he told him.

Soon, my father arrived at the house. I was scared. But since he always treated me well, I wasn't as afraid of him as my sister was. "Come over here," he said to me. "Why did you steal from me? Who sent you? You must never do that. Besides, there are a lot of drunks in the *cantinas*, you should never go inside, even if I'm there. Tell me, who sent you there?"

"Camila." I said.

My father was furious. He got up and went to look for my sister. "Camila! Camila!" Camila didn't answer. She was hiding behind a curtain, listening to everything. My father went on furiously. "You fucking bitch! Sending my own daughter to steal from me in the *cantina*! You shit, you're going to pay for this!" he said.

He finally found Camila. He grabbed her by her braids and pulled her out from where she was hiding. Then he kicked her. Camila fell on the floor and defended herself as best she could. "Let me go, you old fool, or I'll kill you!" she said to him. This made my father furious, and he shouted, angrier than ever, "I'm going to kill you, I'll do it right now, you bitch! You don't deserve to live!" He grabbed an axe that was leaning against the wall. He lifted it up and swung it toward her head with all his might. I screamed and ran to hide in a corner of the room, shaking with fear.

But the axe slipped a little, since my father didn't know how to use it; besides, Camila had moved out of the way, so he cut a piece of her scalp and left a small wound. Camila got up and ran out of the house.

My father took me by the hand and we went out on the street.

He walked, crying silently. Tears rolled down his face. "If only your mother were alive," he repeated, "such things wouldn't happen."

My father began drinking even more. He disappeared for a while. To get back at me, my sister gave me a beating that almost killed me. Soon after that, my father died. Everyone felt sad, because he had always been so kind. We held a three-day wake at my Aunt Antonia's house, and then he was buried in a glass coffin. People from all the nearby villages came to see him.

CAMILA

I was six years old. That's where my memories begin. The first words I remember are: "But she's so small!"

"What do you mean, small? She's big enough! She's already six! She's ready to help me work . . . and that's why I pile it on, so she will learn!"

"But she does the work of a grown woman!"

"Well, that's how you learn, right from the start!"

I'd get up very early, to clean the big leaves we used for making dough. Then I began to knead it. But I made such awful bread I got a beating for it; since it couldn't be sold, they had me make candy twists to sell on the street to make up for what the dough had cost. I did pretty well, and since I had already had one beating, I made sure to sell every last one of those damn candies. I did earn good money.

I finally learned how to knead, to make other sweets and all kinds of *tamales*. I would also make *tortillas* for my brothers to take to the fields to eat. I'd do that early, then come back and sell for the rest of the day, and then at six, when my brothers came home, I'd have the dinner ready. I gave them dinner, and then came the nightly struggle with my sister's younger children, to sing to them and get them to sleep. My sister had a mosquito net. I slept in a hammock with the baby; I had no net. Between the baby and the mosquitos, I didn't sleep all night. And the next day it was back to work.

I learned to slaughter pigs, to milk cows, to make soap and cheese, and to plant different kinds of seeds and harvest them. Every year we would plant rice on an island that was one day's walk away. While we were there I'd get up at five in the morning to clean the rice and feed the workers, at least a hundred of them. They would make piles of rice about half a bushel high. I started cooking it so that it would be ready by seven a.m. when they left for work. That way they could take it along to eat during the day. Then I'd go for water. We had to make a line, because there was a well: whoever arrived first would fill their gourd and then give their place to the next one, and so on.

There was a creek near our house. The creek was full of alligators. There was nothing for them to eat in the creek so they would come out to look for food. They used to carry off our animals. There was a huge one we called "The Monster" because it even went after cows. It had already killed a few of them. We had become used to alligators, and were no longer afraid of them. We knew how to defend ourselves against them. We never let them get close to us. You had to be in front to fight them, because that way they wouldn't attack. Then you'd jump on their back, grab their front feet and turn them belly up. We used to stick a piece of wood in their jaws so they couldn't bite us.

One night an alligator came into the house. I was alone with my brothers and sisters; my sister and brother-in-law had gone out. At midnight, I noticed a horrible stink. I knew it was an alligator, because they all smell.

"Don't move, there's an alligator in here." I said.

We all slept in a big hammock when my sister wasn't home. It was a very dark night and I couldn't see where the alligator was. I tried to guide myself by the smell, but it was impossible, because the whole room stank. Then, taking a chance, I got down from the bed. I tore off a palm branch from the roof of the house and lit it. Then I saw the alligator and I ran toward it. Since alligators are afraid of fire, it ran back to the creek. That one was so big, I think it was "The Monster."

Other times, to keep them at bay and stop them from going after the cows, we put out meat, especially cow's stomachs, hung above the creek. The alligators stayed put, waiting to grab the meat.

Sometimes I was sent to the other side of the creek to bring rennet for making cheese, which we traded for meat, sausage, tomatoes and other things that people came to sell. We would barter for foods.

Since I had a sweet tooth, I liked to steal rice and eggs to trade for fruit; I would keep some for myself and give some to my little nephews and nieces. But some of them were older and if I didn't give them some of the loot they would tell my sister, and there'd be another beating! She hit me with machetes, with sticks, with whatever she found ... or she pulled my hair ... She was no mother to me! Oh, what beatings she gave me!

I was already eight when I heard about Mexico City for the first time. I decided I would go there when I was big. But the people there wear shoes, I told myself, and I don't have any; when I'm bigger, I thought, I'll steal rice to buy myself some shoes!

During those times we were hungry, because the creek had dried up. But there were a lot of shrimp; no one knew how they got there, but all the mothers sent their children to collect them. "Make sure an alligator doesn't eat you; be careful, because they hide in the mud," they told us.

One day I went out to look for shrimp, taking one of Camila's little boys; he was barely a year old. My sister said to me: "Be careful with the baby, don't leave him on the bridge—he'll fall in, or an alligator will get him."

When I got to the swamp, I forgot all about what my sister had told me. I found a lot of children to play with and I sat the baby on the bridge so an alligator wouldn't eat him in case one came out, and because I thought it would be safer. I went to play with the children.

Soon the baby began to cry and I went to see what was happening. I saw that the alligators had begun to come up to sun themselves and that maybe we weren't going to be able to get out. I grabbed the boy and looked all around for where there weren't any alligators, but I was so afraid and I don't know how but I dropped the baby headfirst into the mud, near the alligators . . .

I just stared at him, I didn't know what to do. I started screaming. Then I saw the alligators were lifting their heads up and I had no choice but to throw myself in the mud to either get the baby out or to let the alligators eat me, too, because in any case—I thought—they were going to kill me at home.

I got the baby out as best I could, and I cleaned him off. Since he was covered in mud—in his mouth, eyes, nose, and ears—and he was suffocating. I hit him on the back so he would spit up what he had swallowed. He wasn't crying anymore and I saw that he had swelled up. I screamed and cried. The people came running: "Oh my God! Now your sister will really kill you!" they said.

My sister arrived.

Just as I predicted. To begin with, they gave me a beating that landed me in bed. The baby was very ill. He had broken his back. Another beating. He stayed swollen. Another beating. This went on for ten days. Then he died. The beatings in those days were incredible. The hit me so many times I almost lost my mind.

Time passed. Everything was slowly forgotten. I continued working, going out on the street to sell what we had made: one day bread, another day sweets, or rice pudding, soap, tripe, berries, tamales, watermelon, cantaloupe. Everything sold well and when we were short on money, we traded anything that hadn't been sold for salt, lime, corn, sweet potatoes, or whatever there was that we needed: baby pigs, hens: you see, other people needed the things I offered, and that's how we made deals.

After a day of selling, I'd go home exhausted . . . only to continue working, making dinner . . . and so on, every day.

The beatings came less often, because I worked hard. But later they started again, almost every day, because of my brother-in-law, Pedro.

My brother-in-law was a young country boy, tall, thin, and strong. I had to make his breakfast before he went to work. I complained about it because he was such a big eater and I had to make him so many *gordas*, which are tortillas with beans and *salsa*. And of course, then I had to grind more flour! "Benita, I want more *gordas*!" he'd say to me.

"But I just gave you two!"

"How the hell do you expect me to eat only two!"

I had to grind more flour and I hated him even more. He was very mean to me. He always took Camila's side against me.

One night we were all asleep when I awoke. I felt a hand touching me and poking around in the bed, as if searching for something. Since I slept in the same bed with all my brothers and sisters, I thought it was one of their hands. I grabbed it and realized right away that it was my brother-in-law, Pedro's hand. It was very big, a man's hand.

It was dark. I got up without making a noise and I went to where we kept the knives for killing pigs. I grabbed a knife and climbed back into bed. Soon the hand returned, searching. I grabbed it, and cut it with the knife. I heard a grunt, but he didn't say anything. He left a trail of blood.

The next morning, Pedro wasn't there, because he had left to go to work very early. "Have you seen Pedro?" my sister asked me.

"Yes," I said, "he came to my bed last night."

"What?!"

" . . . and I cut his hand."

Camila glared at me. "And why didn't you scream, why didn't you call me?"

"I didn't think of that."

My sister immediately went to see Pedro at his job. As she left the house, she was grumbling, "Oh, you son of a bitch! You're going to pay for this!"

They had a big fight. Then she came back, furious, and gave it to me, too, beating me hard "because you didn't scream." Pedro didn't come home for ten days. When he returned his hand was bandaged. I had chopped off two fingers.

....

... ...

SHAME

Camila didn't want me to go to school, because I did everything around the house. I did all the chores, and I also earned money from the things I sold on the street. She preferred to have me there all day so she could use and abuse me at her whim.

Sometimes, when I saw the children my age going to school and how they had fun playing, it made me want to go, too. "Camila, I want to go to school," I told my sister.

But Camila pretended not to hear me and so I didn't go, because, of course, it was better for her to keep me home! But once, after I begged and begged, she bought me a primer and she made me learn it by heart. But I also wanted to be with the other children so I could play with them. Then she told me, "If you learn the alphabet in one week, I'll let you be the shepherd in the pastorale."

I was very happy to hear that and sat down to study my alphabet.

It is our custom at Christmas for people to set up a creche in their house. In some room, on top of a table, they place the baby Jesus surrounded by twigs and moss. Then they invite their neighbors over; they sing, they pray and they drink *piñole* and eat *buñuelos*. If someone finds himself in a difficult situation, they take the child to the pastorale as an offering. Then they pay actors to sing to the child and have a big party.

I was about nine years old.

Christmas approached. Every night I would go to practice the pastorale with a group of children. So that my sister would let me be a shepherd, I studied the alphabet as hard as I could. I constantly recited: *be o, bo; de e, de; ge a, ga: bo-de-ga.* I went over and over it until I got it into my head.

Finally the day came for us when we were going to sing. It was in a village called Los Toros, near San Gerónimo.

There was an effeminate man named Melitón who had set up the creche and contracted for the pastorale group to sing to the baby Jesus. I was so excited. My sister had had a beautiful pink linen dress made for me. I already had my shepherd's staff and my flowered hat and I had also memorized the line I was to say to the little Jesus: "I, being the youngest, am the most ashamed; they tell me I have something for the child, but I have nothing."

Everything was ready. My long pink linen dress was perfectly ironed, I knew my line by heart. At last I was going to be a shepherd. I was so excited! The night before the great day I served myself a heaping plate of rice pudding with coconut and went to sleep early.

The next morning I didn't feel too well; my stomach was swollen, but I ignored it and I didn't mention anything to my sister. I got dressed quickly so I would be ready when they came for me.

As we were driving on the highway, I began to feel a twisting pain in my gut, but I just held it in and didn't say anything. Finally we got to Melitón's house. There were already many people waiting for the pastorale to get there so they could start the party.

My stomach was still grumbling, but it was too late to do anything about it. I held it in.

Everyone assembled for the pastorale. The custom is that the shepherds each dance in front of the baby Jesus one by one, reciting a line, and the last one offers him a gift. I was the youngest one in the pastorale, so I had to go first. My stomach kept rumbling. I couldn't take it anymore! I tried hard to hold it in and I danced along the shepherds' line: "I, being the youngest, am the most ashamed . . . " As I started to dance, the pain in my stomach got stronger. I broke out in a cold sweat, but I kept on going, trying to be strong: " . . . they tell me I have to bring something for the child, but I have nothing." I bowed down, and then, wouldn't you know it, it happened!

I felt something warm running down my legs. The people near me began to hold their noses. Others started laughing and they asked someone to take me outside. Melitón came at just that moment. "Oh, little lady! Just look at this! Aren't you ashamed? You say you've brought nothing for the child? Just look what you brought him! Take her to the river!"

I was so angry. I left the house and went down to the river. I took off my new pink linen dress and I washed it. I washed myself and went back to the party, but they didn't want to let me dance and they wouldn't let me eat the little cakes. They shunned me all day.

But the worst was when I went back home. When Camila saw my dress all wrinkled and wet she asked, "What happened to you? Okay, tell me, why did you wash your dress? A man took advantage of you! Tell me who it was!"

"That wasn't it, I swear!"

But my sister didn't give me a chance to explain and gave me a terrible beating. "Tell me who did it to you!" she screamed at me.

"I told you that wasn't it."

"So what then?"

"Well . . . I had an accident!"

Another beating. But Camila still wasn't convinced. She had to ask Melitón what happened. "Yes, it's true," the effeminate man told her, "and the next time she has to go somewhere, don't feed her rice pudding with coconut for dinner . . . "

THE PIG

My life went along as usual: working in the house, taking care of Camila's children, and selling things on the street. I had already lost all hope of leaving town. Since no man had come along to take me away, I had resigned myself to staying.

One day I went to out to the village of El Arenal to sell soap. On the way I met doña Chana la Saligana, with a sow that had just given birth to some piglets. I had grown up around pigs, I knew how to fatten up a pig so that it will have a lot of meat. I liked one of doña Chana's piglets and I said, "I want to buy this chestnut-colored pig. How much is it?"

"No, dear, I can't sell it to you."

"Sell it to me, doña Chana, it's so beautiful."

After we argued about it for a while she said, "Well, okay, give me one *tostón* for her."

"But I don't have any money with me. I'll trade you some soap."

The old woman agreed. I gave her fifty *centavos* worth of soap and took my little pig. I was delighted to take her home. Camila didn't scold me for the exchange I had made.

For a long time I had wanted to buy myself a gold chain. In my town all the girls wore necklaces, earrings, and gold lockets that their parents give them. I dreamed of a gold chain and, since I had no parents to give me one, I thought that by fattening up the little pig I would earn enough money to buy myself a necklace. So the pig was named "Necklace."

I loved her. She would sit next to my grinding stone and I would feed her while I ground corn. I would throw handfuls of corn to her. When the pig finished, she would push me with her snout to let me know that she wanted more. She followed me everywhere. She would be waiting for me whenever I had to get up early. She was the only one who got up with me. I would hug her and scratch her belly. We loved each other very much.

Five months went by.

One day they sent me for some cheese. A storm began as I returned, and when I got to San Gerónimo I saw that the river that overflowed its banks and I couldn't get to my house. I found Camila on the same side of the river; she had gotten the children out and anything else she could. There were many rafts near the river saving the flooded out people. The storm kept on. "Where's my pig?" I asked Camila.

"Well what do you know, poor little pig, we couldn't get her out. I barely had time to grab some clothes."

With that, I jumped into the river with all my clothes on and went looking for my pig, thinking if she drowned I wouldn't get my gold chain. I still hoped that she was stuck on a pole and that I could save her. I was swimming all around in the whirlpools. The river continued to rise . . . and no pig.

When they saw that I hadn't come back, the raft men came to get me. They took me out of the water. I was crying for my pig. Camila tried to calm me down. "Don't cry, baby, I'll buy you another pig." The storm got stronger. The river swept the houses away or tore the roofs off them. The people ran to the church to pray. I went out to watch the storm, and how it carried off the houses.

Later Camila took us to our Aunt Maria's house. We spent the night there. I was thinking about my pig and I couldn't sleep at all. The next day, at lunchtime, we had pork with chile. "Oh, who killed a pig yesterday?" I asked Camila.

"Didn't you know that I went out early? This was all they had left."

Etelvina, one of Camila's daughters, came over to me. She loved me very much because I had always taken care of her. I had raised her almost as if she were my own daughter. When I hit her, she didn't tell Camila, like my other nieces and nephews did. She'd rather have me hit her than her mother. "Beni, when they were killing your little pig, it just made a sound like 'Kwiii, kwiii, and then there was only some hair left . . . '"

"Don't tell me they killed my pig!"

I got up and went to find Camila. "Did you kill my little pig, Camila?"

"No, dear . . . "

"So what pig is all that hair from?" and I pointed to a big pile of hair that came from "Necklace." Camila couldn't deny it. "Well, it's true, we killed her; don't you know the river carried away everything else we had?"

"Yes, I know it took everything away . . . including my gold chain!"

CAMILA VERSUS GUADALUPE

By then I had had enough. I wondered; why doesn't some man come to take me to Mexico City? I want to go where I'll have no desire to return to this land of mine, this ugly land where I have only suffered!

But—how could we get away? Wishes don't make dreams come true. I grew up, and nothing happened! I lost all hope, even forgot my plans to travel to Mexico City. Since no one had come along to take me there . . . well, that was it!

One day I went to the river to wash clothes and I told the other motherless girls that I wanted to leave the village.

"Let's run away!" I said to them. "Let's go where no one will ever find us!"

"How can we run away? Don't be a fool!"

"I'm going to steal something from my house. You take something, too, and we'll go somewhere far away."

"But where? If they come looking for us . . . they'll beat us!"

"They won't. Come on, we can hide, we'll walk at night and sleep during the day."

The girls weren't too sure, but they finally made up their minds.

"What the hell—let's go!"

We started our adventure. We left the village. It was a moonlit night. We forded the river. It was so quiet we could almost hear our hearts beating. We went over the mountain so we wouldn't leave footprints in the sand. I was scared, but since I'd already left the house I refused to go back, and I tried to cheer the other girls up and make them brave.

"Where are you taking me, Benita?" one of them was crying. "It'll be your fault if some man gets us! Then you'll see!"

"Let him get me, what do I care!"

We hadn't been walking long when we heard the pounding of running feet. We quickly hid and stuck out our heads to see who it was and where they were going. We saw that they were our brothers and sisters. Then we got scared, thinking of the beating they were going to give us. They went past without seeing us. But on their way back they found us and whipped us with a lasso until we bled.

That's how we came back to town. The people came out of their houses when they heard us screaming.

"Stop hitting them," they said. "They won't do it again. Right, Benita?"

I was silent.

"Say no, so they'll stop beating you!"

I was silent.

Then they hung me from a rope, and burned my feet with a torch made of corn husks. When I couldn't stand it anymore I said:

"I'll never do it again!"

"Good. Let this be your lesson. Next time we'll kill you!"

I lay down but I couldn't sleep, I was in so much pain. There wasn't one place on my body that didn't hurt. Then the next day it started: "You stupid ass! As young as you are and already into trouble!"

Back to work. Time passed. The adventure was forgotten. But I wanted to escape more than ever. One day a circus came to town. I made friends with some boys who worked the trapeze. "I want to be a tumbler in the circus and run away with you!" I said to them.

"So come on, let's go!"

"Really?"

"Really!"

The day the circus left I escaped from my house, but someone saw me and ran to tell my sister. "Oh my God!" she said. "The man of the house is gone!" She found someone to help her and ran to get me. She brought me home, but that time she didn't beat me. She treated me very well, but I knew it wasn't because she loved me, but because my work supported the whole family and she needed me there. I hated her!

In town there was a rather wealthy old man who heard about what had happened. "I'll marry Benita." he said. "She's a good girl and she's pretty and young, and since she doesn't want to live at home anymore, I'll be her fiance."

The old man was around sixty years old, and a widower eleven times over. He had about thirty children.

One day at the river he spoke to me. He called me over and said, "Benita, I'm going to marry you." He scared me. "Get away from me, if they see me with you they'll beat me!" I told him.

"No one is going to beat you. Just the opposite, they'll let you marry me. I'm going to ask them today. Then we'll get married and I'll give you everything you want. Everything I have will be yours. You'll be rich. I'll buy you shoes, dresses, whatever you want. Say you'll marry me! You know how women love me because I'm good to them. It's my bad luck that they all died, but that doesn't mean you will, too."

Then, because I had heard that the old man killed his wives, and that was why he married a new one every year, I said, "Look, you're not going to get me, too. First of all, I don't want your money, and in the second place, you're an old man."[1]

"But if they beat you at home, why don't you marry me?"

"I said no!"

I left him standing there. The old man went to find a woman to tell me I should marry him. She convinced me. I told him I'd get married. The old guy was happy again when he saw I had accepted. He went to see my sister right away. He talked to her. My sister called me over. She asked me if I wanted to get married, so she could give me away at once. She says to me, "Do you know how old you are?"

"No."

"Well, you're about thirteen. But if you want to get married, of course I'll say yes."

"Fine, I'll get married."

"So get ready for your wedding."

And that's how it was arranged. I didn't plan a thing. Time went by and no wedding. The old man kept after me, he gave me presents, he promised me a mountain of things, but I didn't love him, so I didn't say anything. "When are we going to get married, Benita?" he would ask me.

"Soon." I'd say.

I thought to myself: if I marry this guy, I'll run away with the money he gives me.

The days went by and the wedding was planned. Everyone in town knew I was going to marry him and they all asked me, "Benita, are you really going to marry that mean old man, as cheap as he is? Don't you know he kills his wives so he can marry new ones? And he has so many kids! Don't get married, don't be a fool!"

"But they already promised me to him!" I said. "And we don't have the money to pay back the money he has spent!"

"It doesn't matter, don't do it, tell him to go to hell!"

After being told the same thing so many times that I decided to do it. The next day I told him, "I'll never marry you!"

"What do you mean you won't marry me? I already have your dress. Besides, your family doesn't have any money. How are you going to pay me back for what I've spent?"

"Whatever happens, I'm not marrying you, you old wretch!"

"Well, I'm going to tell your sister right now."

He left. He said all kinds of things to her. They called for me. "So you're not getting married?" my sister said.

"No!"

"Why? Because he's old, or is it that you have a boyfriend?"

I said nothing.

"Tell me why not! How can we get out of it now? How are we going to pay him back? He's given you rings, a gold necklace, everything you wanted. Didn't you tell me you would work day and night just to buy yourself a necklace? Well, now give it all back to him!"

I gathered up everything. I threw it all on the ground. "Fine, but this isn't the end of it." the old man said. "Everyone knew today was my wedding day!"

He left the house, furious. I knew he was going to plan something against me. So I didn't lose any time. I made a friend write a letter for me to my sister Guadalupe, who was in Acapulco. I told her what had happened. I told her to come get me.

A few days later Guadalupe came. Camila was surprised. "Hey, what are you doing here?" she said. When she realized why my other sister was there, she got mad. She didn't want to let me go. My sisters argued. When she realized the problems I was having, Guadalupe decided we would leave together, no matter what. My sisters started to fight again. "Benita doesn't want to live here anymore, so I'm taking her with me."

"But how can you take her, when I need her here?"

"Maybe you do, but I'm not going to let you marry her off to that old man."

They went on and on; Guadalupe, about how I was going with her, Camila, about how she wouldn't let me go. Then Guadalupe got mad. "Whatever it takes, she's going with me!" she said. Camila stood up and grabbed a knife. "I'll kill you before you take her!"

I ran over to the machetes and got two, one for Guadalupe and another for me. I stood very close to her side. When he saw that, Pedro got up from where he was and slowly went over to the machetes. He grabbed his. My sisters kept yelling. "Don't think you scare me, Camila. Benita's going with me and that's that."

"You're not going to go, are you, my girl?" Camila said to me. "Yes I am!"

"Then we'll all go to hell here, but Benita's not leaving this house!"

"That's bullshit! We'll see if she doesn't leave . . . I came to get her and I'm not leaving without her!"

With the machetes ready, Guadalupe and I walked over to the door. Camila tried to attack us, but Guadalupe jumped at her with the machete. "And what the fuck are you doing, why aren't you helping me?" Camila said to Pedro, my brother-in-law. He was just standing there looking; he didn't know what to do. "Are you going to let this bitch take Benita?"

Pedro lunged at us, but we swung the machetes out at him. Then we ran through the corral, to where the horses were. The moon was out that night. I tried to get out through a gate in the corral, but I was scared and I was running and I didn't notice, so I fell against the barbed wire. Camila and Pedro were coming up behind us.

"Run!" Guadalupe said. I went through the fence, tearing my dress. Camila came after me, screaming curses and threatening us with the knife. "We'll see each other again, motherfucker!"

"Go to hell, bitch!"

That's how my sisters said goodbye.

---

[1] The old man finally married Rosita, a close friend of mine. When I went back to the village some time later, I found out that Rosita was very sick; they said it was from a kick in the chest that he had given her. A few days later she died. The old man got married again, to my niece Carlotita, and soon he left her with a daughter; he didn't kill her because Carlota fought back. Later she left him.

I HAVE SHOES!

We walked all that night, because we we afraid the old man would realize that I had left and come looking for me with soldiers. But he didn't even hear about it until much later.

We got to Acapulco. My sister bought me some shoes. She fixed me up. At the beginning, she treated me well. But within a few days . . . oh, what I life I led!

She told me to do the ironing, and since I had never seen anyone iron, of course I burned the clothes. A whipping for that!

But what do I care, I have shoes!

They told me to make soup. But since I didn't know how, I burned that, too. Another whipping!

So let them do it, I have shoes!

Starch the clothes, they said; but because we didn't have starch in my village, it was a mess! Another whipping!

But let them whip me, I have shoes!

They didn't have any of those things in my village, I seemed to deserve a whipping every hour of the day. What a life I led!

I started to make friends in Acapulco. "Benita," they would say to me, "why don't you have a boyfriend?"

"Because no one is in love with me!"

"But there are so many boys! Someone told me he thinks you're very beautiful."

"Tell me who it was! He really told you that?"

"He did, he really did!"

Could I really be pretty?— I asked myself.

The next day my sister went out to buy something. I got dressed. I put on lipstick; I didn't know how to do it and I looked horrible, but my friend had told me, "Put on some make-up, so when he goes by, you'll look pretty." So I made up my face as well as I knew how.

The young man walked by my house with my friend. I went outside to watch them. When he saw me he came over. I ran back to my house and stood watching through the window, through a crack in the glass. When he had left I started crying and said to myself, "Is that what it's like to have a boyfriend? Because I guess I'm his girlfriend now. What's he going to say to me? I was waiting all day for them to go by! And finally they did!"

He was about fifteen years old or so, I'm not sure. I was crazy with happiness thinking that now I had a boyfriend, but I also thought about the whipping that would come when . . . But no, I hadn't even spoken with him! And that's what I thought it was to have a boyfriend!

The next day, I went to the *zocalo*, the central plaza, to buy some things, as I usually did. The first person I saw was the young man. He walked up to me. "Señorita," he said, "what a pleasure it is to see you, to speak with you!" I didn't answer him; I didn't know what to say. I looked down and kept walking, thinking that people would see me and would tell my sister that I was with a boy. He kept talking to me. I was quiet. Then I answered him, because he kept on saying things to me. "Well, what do you want?"

"I want to be your love, your boyfriend, because I love you with all my heart."

"Well I do too!"

"So, we're lovers?"

"I guess we are! But stop looking at me, my sister has a bad temper and she won't let me leave the house."

"So how can we see each other?"

"I'll tell you later, but you have to go now, I can't let anyone see us!"

He left. I walked along, happy that I had a boyfriend. From that day on I went out often to buy things, anything, because he would wait for me on the corner. We would just look at each other; we'd never say a word. I would go in and out of the house on any pretext. Since I wouldn't talk to him, he wrote me a letter, but I couldn't read, so I just kept it. I was afraid that whoever read me the letter wouldn't tell me what it really said.

The days went by and I didn't answer the letter. Then I went out to see him so he'd tell me what it said. I got a chance to speak to him. "What did you say in your letter?" I said.

"But haven't you read it?"

"No, because I don't know how to read!"

He didn't say anything. We sat for a while, in silence, without looking at each other. Then he said, "And to think I loved you!"

He said goodbye. A few days went by and he didn't come back. I was desperate to see him. My eyes were swollen from crying so much. More days went by and nothing! Then I went to see a friend and I told her what had happened. She said, "Silly! Don't you know why he never came back? It's because you can't read!"

"But why is it my fault they never taught me at home! I'll tell you what they taught me: I know how to make soap, tortilla dough, to grow corn, to split wood and to sell things."

"Yes, but he doesn't care about that, if you're stupid. Everyone around here can read, didn't you know that? We're all literate!"

When I got home I cried, for my boyfriend had left me because I couldn't read. Time went by. I forgot about it. But one day I saw him on the beach; he had another girl on his arm. If I knew how to read, I thought, that would be me on his arm. When would I learn? One day, when my sister was in a good mood, I told her, "I want to learn to read."

"What do you want that for?" she answered. "What you should do is learn to work, so you can support yourself. You have to learn to wash, to iron, and to make food so when you get married, your husband won't call you lazy and say, 'Didn't they teach you anything at home?'"

I did everything they asked, eagerly, but I had no experience, and I did everything badly. Then the beatings rained down.

I was older now, and I wanted to read. I went to see a friend who knew how and I asked her to teach me. She said she would. She got me on the *a e i o u*'s. "You're going to learn these letters," she said, "When you're ready, come back and tell me what they are." I studied them for days and days and I didn't learn even one. My friend insisted that I recite them from memory. "Now I'm going to give you all the ABC's and you're going to learn those, too. Then you come back and recite your lesson." A few days later she came back and I still didn't know anything. "Read it again, until you can give it to me by memory," she said.

Finally I learned it. Then I bought myself a notebook and I learned to write, but since I wasn't really determined to learn I didn't pay too much attention and mostly just left it alone. A few days later I took the notebook again and started to read more and that's how I learned to put letters together. I would write on the sand. I wrote my name and other simple things and it was easy.

I had another suitor, an Arab named Cassis. He was the owner of a store, and handsome and rich, but I thought that he would only want someone who could read. I started practicing more, but I was already so upset, the letters wouldn't stay in my memory and I couldn't learn. I started to act silly with the rich man. He quickly saw that I didn't know how to read. "Why don't you learn to read?" he said one day. "That way when I write you letters you can answer them." I was so ashamed I ran away. I didn't go by his store anymore, because I didn't want him to see me. Then he came looking for me. He saw me and started talking to me; he asked me to live with him. He would give me things, he said. He couldn't marry me because I had no money; I was poor and he was rich and his family wouldn't permit it. I started to cry. "Why won't you come with me?" he said. "Who are you afraid of?"

I didn't say anything. I went home, in despair, thinking that if I went with him he would leave me later, like rich men always did. But my aspirations were great. I wanted to have money so I would be appreciated by the people who dressed well, who have so many clothes. I thought if I went with Cassis, I would had a lot of clothes, since he was the owner of a store and would give me everything, but then . . . off with you!—would come next.

No, no, no! Then he came back. He offered me everything all over again. "Benita, what do you say, will you come with me?" I was thinking that no one would ever say I was pretty. I had heard from my own friends' lips, "If you had some nice dresses, you would be the prettiest girl in the whole port." "So, are we going?" If I did, everyone would say, "Ah, there goes Cassis' lover." "Benita, tell me, are you coming with me or not?"

"No! I'd rather marry a poor man who loves me, and you only want me to be your lover. I hate you! Take your money and get out of here. I'm going to marry a poor man who won't leave me, who will love me, who will make me happy."

"But who could give you more than I could!"

I went home, thinking that I would never get married, not to a poor man or a rich man either, not until a stranger came to take me far away from here, so that if things went badly, people wouldn't tease me, and my family would never know.

MY LITTLE DARK GIRL

I turned fifteen. I started to develop. I weighed one hundred and twenty pounds and I was lively. I started falling in love with everyone, rich and poor. I had boyfriends and more boyfriends. I didn't want to be a slave to work anymore, I was so bored by it. What shall I do? Send everyone to hell and love no one! I had some friends who said to me, "If I were like you, I'd be in love with every man who courted me; but you're so foolish, you don't even pay attention to them. If you did, we could go to the beach together. He'd buy us ice cream and I'd stroll around with you."

"Okay, I'll choose one of them to be my boyfriend."

"Which one?"

"Enrique Estrada."

"Oh, look at the one she picks!"

"So who, then?"

"Someone with money."

"You tell me who I should pick. I'll tell you who they are. There are three candidates, walking around the *zocalo* together."

"Who are they?"

"Pepe Cassis, Tomás Lepe, and Enrique."

"Well, Pepe's the best. Do you know what it would be like to be the girlfriend of a rich man, who owns his own store? He'll take you everywhere and the rich women will stop and stare at you, walking around with a rich man. They'll all be envious. "I can't believe my eyes, look who he's with, he's walking arm in arm with a poor girl!" they'll say.

"Yes, but I think Tomás Lepe would be a better choice."

"You fool, don't you know he has no money? Anyway, he's a pig butcher. What can you expect from that? What you should do is find someone who'll really make the rich women burn, someone who will make them see that poor people can have rich boyfriends, too."

"But you don't know what he wants me to do."

"What?"

"He wants me to go live with him. And as you know, men take girls away from their families and give them a baby and then they leave them."

"Yes, but if you do it right, when they leave you, they'll leave you with a nice house," one of my friends said. "I'm going to get one of them to take me away with him, so I'll have everything I need for a while and then people will say: she lived with a rich man."

"Well not me! I'm going to choose Tomás Lepe, because he didn't ask me to live with him. Besides, he said he was going to be a sailor on the next ship that comes in and when he comes back we'll get married, that he'll bring money and then I'll be happy."

Everyone laughed at me and said that if I became Tomás' girlfriend they'd never speak to me again. "I don't care, I'm going to be his girlfriend!"

"But you don't even love him!"

"So what? At least people won't be talking about me, they won't be dragging my name through the mud."

"Fine, but don't try to be our friend!"

I told Tomás I wanted to be his girlfriend. Soon after that he left on a ship. He got as far as Manzanillo, because the boat he was on didn't go to the United States, which was where he wanted to go to seek his fortune so that we could get married. He returned very soon. He was sad. He told me what had happened and said that he would just keep being a pig-butcher until there was a boat that would take him somewhere he could seek his fortune. I was still his girlfriend. Days went by, then weeks, and no boat. Then we started arguing. I told him I was going to go back to my family because my brother was very sick and he didn't have money for the medicine and I had to work to earn enough for his treatment. "And what kind of work are you going to do?" he asked me.

"I don't know yet!"

We parted. He never returned, and I never thought about him again, because I didn't love him—I didn't love anyone!

Soon after that I started up with Enrique Estrada. One day he invited me to go to an orchard. I took some of my little nieces along. We spent the whole time at the orchard picking mangoes. When we got home, one of my nieces told my cousin that Enrique had kissed me. This wasn't true, and anyway, a woman who lets herself be kissed is lost because later men don't want her; they say she slobbers over anyone in sight. I ran looking for Enrique. I found him shaving himself in a doorway. "Come with me, Enrique, quickly!"

"What is it?"

"Just come, I said!"

And in front of my cousin I said, "Enrique, they say you kissed me and held me when we were at the orchard." Enrique looked down. "Neither I nor Benita even thought about doing something like that . . . " he said. "But it's your own daughter who wants to entrap me and that's why she's telling false stories about Benita . . . "

My sister had just come back from Mexico City and had left me with a cousin who was the wife of a deputy and had a daughter my age. The daughter was secretly in love with Enrique Estrada. We had many parties in the house, and she had to introduce me into society just as if I were part of the family. I learned to dance. I went to the rich people's dances. All the boys said I was pretty, and asked where I was from. "I am from San Gerónimo," I would say to them.

"Who are your parents?"

"I don't have parents."

"But who were they, what were their names?"

"My father's name was Genaro Lacunza, the richest man in town in his time."

"Oh yeah? And how are you related to General Albino Lacunza?"

"I'm his niece, but ever since we became poor he won't recognize me."

"But you should go see him, ask him to help you. Aren't you related to Rodolfo Neri, the governor of Chilpancingo?"

"Yes."

"And who is Antonio Sosa to you?"

"He is my cousin."

"Wow! Why don't you go see them? You could really be somebody!"

"No, I don't want anyone feeling sorry for me."

"But really, you should, don't you understand . . . "

"Yes I do, but I said no!"

"Do you have any boyfriends?"

"No, and I don't plan to have any. Not because I don't want them, but because everyone thinks badly of me."

The dance ended. I had learned how to talk in society. Now people paid attention to me. They held dances at my cousin's house every Sunday. I had many suitors but I never had a boyfriend again, because they all seemed like they wanted me to sleep with them, and then I wouldn't be worth anything, and since the only thing I had in life was being a virgin, and that was why they paid attention to me, I thought that as soon as I lost that, no one would bother with me. I thought that in order to receive attention I had to guard my only capital, which was my virginity. But I was so excited about going to Mexico City, I thought it was my only hope for being happy, so I went without boyfriends.

One day a man introduced himself to me. My cousin was in love with him, but neither the man nor I knew it. He talked to me and I told my cousin about it. She was furious. "You're shameful! Ever since you came to live with us no man pays attention to me. I don't know what they see in you; your feet are so ugly they look like elephant's feet, and your legs are more like table legs. What's so beautiful about you? You don't dress well, while look at me! I'm the deputy's daughter. You have all of four dresses, and I have dozens. My father goes to Mexico City and brings me back expensive dresses . . . "

"Look," I answered, "I can't say what I really want to, because I am in your home. But all I will say is, you can't make a silk purse from a sow's ear." I grabbed my things and ran from the house. I went to see a friend and told her what had happened and asked her for a corner of her house to sleep in, because I would never go back to my cousin's. "You really should go back," she said.

"No, not until my sister sends for me," I answered. "Anyway, she already told me they were going to send for me soon, and you know, she's in Mexico City now, and that's where my future is. I'll get married there, and . . . "

"Okay, okay, you can stay here!"

So I stayed there, but wondered what I would do, not knowing how I would eat.

Soon my cousin came to the house. She asked me to forgive her, she said she was angry because no one was in love with her, even though she was a deputy's daughter, but that she had accepted it. That she really was in love with Enrique, but she would wait for him to court her. She said it wasn't my fault that he spoke to me. "Come on, let's go home, you know we all love you."

"I am never going back to your house. Stop bothering me, I never want to see you again. You have insulted me. I thank you for everything you've done for me. I was very happy in your house, but now I've realized how important it is to have parents. I will look for my independence. I'll go find a rich man who will take me away with him . . . "

My cousin ran off, crying.

The next day I went to Cassis' store. I found out he was sick. I asked his sister what was wrong with him he and she said it was a fever. Then I met a friend and told her who I was going to see. "But don't you know what everyone's saying?" she said. "They say Pepe has tuberculosis from being with so many women."

Now what could I do? Just cry again! I went to see a friend who lived nearby. I told her what had happened. There was one son in that family. We started talking and since I now knew how to carry on a conversation and to speak better than when I first got there, we talked for a long time. I went back to the house where I was staying.

The next day the boy came by. "Benita, my mother sent me to bring you to our house for dinner."

"Okay, let's go."

They had already decided that the boy would be my husband. "Anyway," they thought, "there's no one else who wants her; we'll talk her into it when she gets here." And, in fact, the two of them did convince me. I said yes, even though I didn't love him. But I had two little boys with me from the house I was staying at, and they understood everything. They went to tell their mama, but when she came to rescue me I had already gone with him to another house.

His mother promised me we would be married the very next day, and I, always the believer, well, I had no choice, there was nothing else to do. The next day the people were saying: "You know, Benita ran off with that woman's son. Poor little girl, look who she decided to go off with. Everyone loved her so much . . . and she had some good suitors, rich ones . . . the fool! What a stupid move!"

My husband was a court reporter. He made enough for everyday things, but he had to support his mother, too, and the whole family, and he didn't make enough for that. Then one day his mother said to me, "Benita, why don't you work, too? After all, you know how. I'll set you up with a stand in the market and you'll have money so you can help your husband. Besides, you're going to be a mother soon . . . "

"What? I'm going to be a mother? Whose mother?"

"You're pregnant!"

"I am not!"

"You're already five months along, dear!"

"How do you know?"

"What do you mean, how? I just know!"

I ran off to cry. When my husband came home I told him what his mother had said to me, that I was pregnant, that I was going to have a baby and that I had to go to work. "Yes, you're going to be a mother."

"But why didn't you tell me before?"

"I didn't want to frighten you."

"But as for working . . . " he said, "I won't allow it! We'll get away from my mother, she's the one causing the problems, and then you can have your baby in peace. My mother is too old to be creating problems like that . . . "

"What do you think we should do?"

"Leave here as soon as possible!"

We went out looking for a room to move into, where his mother wouldn't bother us anymore. We found one. When we returned to my mother-in-law's house, my husband said, "Mother, my wife and I are leaving you."

"What? Why?"

"Because all you do is bother her and she can't stay here in her state. I'll come back to see you. I'll give you money for food . . ."

My mother-in-law got angry. "This woman won't stop until she takes you away from me! Besides, you're not really her husband. She's only living with you. When you leave my side, it will only be to be with your wife."

Then my mother-in-law picked up a whip and tried to beat me. "I'm not his wife," I answered her, "because you locked me in here and tricked me and now I am a fallen woman. The time went by and we didn't marry . . . but I don't even care. I don't love your son. He's very ugly. He looks like an insect. Everyone tells me to leave him, that I have no future with him . . . "

"You see, my son, I told you! I told you this woman wouldn't be faithful to you. Forget about about finding her a house. Stay here with your mother, who's the only one who will look out for you."

The man started wailing. "But I loved her so much!" he said between sobs. "What should I do, mother? And I was ready to be the father of a little boy or a little girl. I had thought that if it was a boy I would buy him an aviator suit and if it was a girl, I would dress her with all the luxuries of the rich . . . what a disgrace! The baby's mother doesn't love me, and being the father of a child who is a product of love . . . that wasn't really love! Mother, it's all your fault! Come with me, my woman, we're going to get married. I want to give my name to my child . . . you will be married . . . "

I was thinking that if I married him I would have to put up with his mother, and that's why I refused do it. "I don't want to get married," I told him. "I'm only waiting to give birth so I can go to my sister in Mexico City."

His mother was happy to hear that. "You see how she is?" she said. "Do you hear that she's just waiting for the time to leave you? And you're still thinking about marrying her . . . you see how right I am, my son?"

Mother and son continued arguing. I listened without saying a word. Then I made my decision. "Look, señora, it's clear I don't love your son. Don't you remember he was never my boyfriend? I didn't mean a thing to him. You were the one who told me, 'Tomorrow you're going to marry."

"Well that's why I didn't want you to marry him, I knew this would happen. My son is not going to marry—"

"I don't want to marry him at all," I interrupted her. "What I want is to get away from here."

"When?"

"Right now!"

"But where will you go? You're five months pregnant and your child won't have a name."

"Oh, so what! I didn't have a father or a mother either!"

"Fine, so get out of here, now!"

"You better believe I'm going!"

I grabbed my clothing and ran, without knowing where. I walked around, I didn't know where to go. When I had calmed down a little, I went to see a woman who had a daughter away at school and I asked her if I could stay in her house. She agreed and I moved in with her. She was a washerwoman. I would help her with the laundry to earn my food. The birth was coming near and I didn't have a cent, so I went to see the midwife. She said she would help me, but I had to give her half the money in advance, because, as she told me, "how are you going to pay me afterward?"

Meanwhile, the pain got worse. Finally I convinced her I

would get the money to her later. "But how do you know how much it will cost?"

One day I started feeling bad at about five in the morning. Happily an ugly little baby girl was born who looked like a dark monkey. How ugly my daughter was! I kissed her. "You see," the midwife told me, "if you had gone with Pepe you would have produced a good child. You would have had a light-skinned daughter, pretty, and with money. And you don't even have enough money to pay me. But I'll go see the father . . . "

"Yes, he'll pay you!"

"Oh, that's what you think! I already went to see him!"

"What did he say?"

"He said that since you abandoned him, he wouldn't give you one cent! Fine, I just hope you don't forget what you owe me."

A month later, the baby's father came to see her. "I paid the midwife," he said. From now on, I will give you one *tostón* a day."

It went on for three months. Then one day I said, "Aren't you going to buy shoes for your daughter?"

"No," he said. "Because I'm going to marry the daughter of the woman whose house you're staying at, and she told me if I kept giving you money she would stop loving me . . . and since you don't love me, well . . . not one more cent!"

I went to see my cousin and told her everything that had happened. She scolded me. I asked her to lend me a little money so I could start making candies or bread. She gave me five *pesos*. I started my work. It went well; I sold all the bread I made. The little girl was five months old. I started to save some money. Then I thought that if I went home to my village, I could make more money. I decided to go and I went.

My family was alarmed because I arrived with a baby. But after all, they said, they didn't have to love it. I started the hard life of a street vender. I got my business going. I bought beer and went to an army barracks and well, nobody sold more than I did, because it was illegal to sell beer and I sold it for a good price.

One day I woke up and saw a pimple on my daughter's chin. That day my sister Camila was planning to slaughter a pig. "What, you're going to kill the little pig?" I asked her.

"Of course! Why?"

"Because my daughter has a pimple on her chin and if you kill the pig, she'll get lockjaw and die."

"Well let that ugly little thing die! I don't know why you had to mess around with that man; he must have pig's blood in him himself. In our family, our blood is real enough!"

I had to go to a town four hours away by foot from San Gerónimo to buy the beer, so I begged my sister not to kill the pig. I told her I would give her the profit she would have gotten from it when I got home. She agreed to my promise, but as soon as I left, she killed the pig.

My little girl scratched the pimple on her face. It started to bleed and her face swelled up so much she couldn't even cry.

I was starting to feel uneasy in the village. I felt like something was happening. I felt desperate! I couldn't decide what to buy. Finally I made my purchase and put it on my head and carried it that way so I could save the price of renting a burro. The trip is four hours going and four coming back, on foot, but it took even longer on the way back because of my load.

My daughter didn't run out to greet me when I got home. I thought something had happened. I went inside. Everything was silence. "Where is my little darkie?" I asked my sister.

"Just calm down so I can tell you!"

"Okay, tell me, what happened to her, where is she?"

"She's sick!"

I ran to her and lifted up the mosquito net. When I saw her, she couldn't even open her eyes. I started to cry. I remembered my aunt was a doctor; she would cure her. I went to see her.

"Auntie, I have my sick little girl here, won't you cure her for me?" I said.

"Let me look at her."

After she examined her she said, "She's very ill; there's no cure for this. It's better just to let her die. Why do you want such an ugly girl, anyway? I won't cure her!"

I left, thinking how I didn't have a cent because I had spent everything on my purchase and I couldn't go out to sell it because I had to watch my daughter who was so sick . . . then I remembered a general who had once said he loved me. I went to see him. I told him what was happening. "Well okay," he said, "but you will have to come live with me after. We'll get a doctor, the one with the wooden leg, to cure your daughter, because the doctor from the Batalon isn't here. He'll charge me two hundred *pesos* and I'll pay it, but you are coming with me!"

"Fine, I'll go; I want my to see my daughter get well."

"Well then, let's go see the doctor."

The doctor examined her, took a razor blade and opened up her chin. He washed it with flower water and bandaged it. I went home, thinking that now I had to go live with the general, and without wanting to! But there was no other way, I would have to go. A few days later he came to see me. "How are you? I'm waiting for the day that you'll come live with me. But I want only you, not your daughter. What would people say? Find someone to leave her with, and I'll give you money so she'll take care of her."

"Fine, that's what I'll do," I said.

The day arrived when I had promised to go. I started crying. I have never loved any man, I thought, and I don't love him either. When will I love a man? Maybe never, because they all want me only for my body; all of them have taken advantage of my sad situation. Why couldn't a man fall in love with me who I could love, too?

A few days after that the general told me we were going to Mexico City. "But you're not bringing your daughter, you'll leave her here."

"No, I can't!"

"Why do you care, you can always come back to see her."

"Okay then, it's all right."

I went to see my daughter. I kissed her. "Soon I'll be back to see you, my baby," I told her. "I'm going to Mexico City, where I always wanted to go."

We left at five in the morning. I was thinking on the way that I would never be back to see my daughter. What could I do?

Then something happened; I don't know why but the general had to go off to give some orders somewhere and he left me with his assistant. I told him my situation and asked him to let me go back home. "Fine, but what do I tell the general?" he said.

"Tell him you didn't see me go."

" . . . Only if you give me something."

"What should I give you?"

"Money, of course! I know you have some."

"I'll give you whatever you want."

"How much is that?"

"How much do you want?"

"Well, I want whatever you'll give me."

"Here are fifty *pesos* then."

"No, that's too little."

"But I only have one hundred . . . "

"Well, hand them over!"

I gave them to him and left for home. I raced the horse so fast that I got overheated and fainted. When I woke up again I hurried on my way.

The army horse I had was a good runner, so I arrived before they could catch up with me. "Benita's here—" people were saying, "what happened to her?"

I was sad with a pain that no one understood, and I could not explain it to anyone. I was like a mad person, not knowing what would become of me. I was so ashamed that I didn't leave my house for days. I had used up the few *centavos* I had left and I was afraid he would come for me and beat me, so I stayed home. Luckily the old soldier never came. My fear disappeared the same time as my money. Now what to do? Then a woman came to see me. "Benita, this has happened because you don't go to church. Why won't you go to confession? Go to church and confess everything."

"Fine, I'll go see if that changes my luck."

I went to church, but I didn't confess anything because I didn't know what to say to the priest. I saw him and I thought, he has money, and the horrible things that happened to me never happened to him. I hated him. If there really were a God, I thought, I would not have suffered so much. I left the church, angry at God. I said to myself: Why won't you give me a good man who loves me, someone who will take me away from here, me and my daughter? What, don't you know all the things that have happened to me? Why do other people have money? Why don't you give some to poor people, too?

Then the woman came back. "Did you go to confession?"

"No!"

"Now you'll see where the devil takes you," she said.

She frightened me and I began praying at night before I went to sleep. About midnight I felt that the devil really would take me away. I felt the bed flying and going around in circles. Then I promised myself I would never pray again, because praying only brings bad dreams.

A few days later I fought with my sister and she threw me out of the house. I didn't have a cent. People were saying horrible things about me. "She was always so lively," they said. "Who knows why things turned out so badly. Poor thing! Her own family doesn't even want her. But then she . . . why didn't she go with the general? He had taken her with him, what more did she want?"

"You see, she's bad luck," others said.

"No, some people just don't know when enough is enough."

"Yes, that's the truth."

So my sister ran me out of the house and I went to a hut with a straw roof that was on the edge of town. The little house was off by itself. It started to rain. The owner said she had another. I went to see it and I told her to give it to me, that I would take care of it. "What is this 'I'll take care of it' business! If you want it, give me seventy-five *pesos*."

"I'll give you a *tostón* in advance."

"Fine."

I went to pick up my daughter and took her to the hut. I had nothing to sleep on or to cover myself with. I got some dresses that the general had bought me and put them on top of me when I slept.

Everything was so sad! I was alone, with my daughter and no money.

THE *MEZCAL* SELLER

One day a *mezcal* seller came by. I had an idea. I went to see him and asked him to give me a carafe of *mezcal* on credit. He did. Back home I told everyone I knew that I had some good *mezcal*, and why didn't they buy some from me. "Are you sure it's really good?" they asked me.

"I'm sure, really."

"Okay, we'll be there tonight."

No one came that night, but the next morning they came, since it's the custom for the workers to have a drink before they go to work. "How much is a quarter carafe?"

"One *tostón*."

I gave them a quarter. They liked it. "This is great," they said, "and tonight we'll be back with some friends, because this *mezcal* is truly good stuff."

Since I knew they would be back that night, and that I'd sell a lot, I threw some warm water into the *mezcal* and then, of course, it wasn't good anymore. That night they returned. "Give us a half." I gave it to them and they took a small taste. "This is awful!" they said. "It's no good! It's pure water! Benita, why did you put water in the *mezcal*? It was so good! Let's go somewhere else. You know where? To Adela's. She sells the good stuff."

"So let's go!"

They all left, leaving me alone with my *mezcal*. Now what to do? Tomorrow the *mezcal* seller would be back to take the *mezcal* that's left . . . and he wasn't going to want it. He came in the afternoon. "*Señora*, I've come for the money or the *mezcal*."

"I haven't sold any," I said. "It's still full."

"I figured you weren't cut out for it. This work isn't for just anyone. Well, give it to me, then. Wait . . . did you add water to this?"

I kept quiet. My silence made him think, and then taste the *mezcal*. "Of course you didn't sell any, if you put in this much water!"

I didn't know what to say. "I'm telling you, if you light a match it won't even burn. And what are you going to do now? How will you pay me for the *mezcal*?"

"How? Very simple: I will be your woman. It doesn't matter,

all I am is merchandise for men. And through it all, I will never love you!"

The man was surprised to hear me talk like that. "Why do you say that?"

"Because how else can I pay you?"

"Yes, but . . . no, not that; I am a gentleman, and I will never bother you again."

He went away. "Goodbye!"

"Goodbye!"

As he was leaving he turned around. "Have you eaten?" he asked.

"No."

He was shaking his head. "What a girl!" he was saying. "What a girl!"

He came back that night. I was asleep on the floor when he knocked. "Who is it?" I asked.

"It's me, the *mezcal* seller."

I was scared. "What do you want?"

"Wake up, I have your dinner."

"But I'm already asleep."

"Get up, I need you; besides, I have a present for you."

"Okay, I'm coming."

I was afraid, but ready for anything. I got up, thinking, what this man wants is for me to pay him for the *mezcal*.

He came in. I lit a match. "Don't you have light?" he asked me.

"No."

"Why not?"

"Because I have no lamp, only candles, and right now not even those."

"Aren't you afraid?"

"I'm not afraid of anything."

"Not even of God?"

"Even less! I've asked him to change my luck so many times and he doesn't pay attention to me."

"Well it's going to change now. Take this."

I saw him take some money out of his pocket. I don't know how much it was. He gave it to me.

"Take this, and tomorrow go to the market and buy whatever you want. And now to sleep; tomorrow will be another day. Good night."

What did he want from me?—I thought. Nothing, but he'll make me go away with him because I owe him for the *mezcal*. What will people say tomorrow when they see me in the market buying milk for my daughter?

I went out very early the next day with my head held high. I bought ten *centavos* worth of milk and paid with paper bills. People were staring at me. I kept walking. I bought meat and some other things, thinking, the *mezcal* seller will get his money's worth from me one way or another.

He did not come the next day or the day after that. I was waiting. Nothing. What could have happened to him? This is good, I thought, at least I got some money. How will I pay him for what he did for me? And he didn't say a word about it! I held my daughter close. "What a good man he is, my dear," I told her. Where could he be? He wasn't from around here so I didn't know how to find him. He's a good man, I thought. I'll go live with him if he wants me to; I'll be his woman. When will he be back?

One day I was sitting in the doorway nursing my baby when I heard someone saying to me, "Good morning! How have you been?"

"Very well!"

It was the *mezcal* seller. "Are you really well?"

"Yes, really."

"I have a present here for your daughter."

What could it be? Shoes? A dress? What a surprise! I took it, a little afraid. "If you want to come with me, I will take you wherever you want," he said.

"I'll think about it." (I knew all the presents and money would have to be paid back somehow.) "Where would we go?"

"To my village. Come on, let's go, we're leaving today."

"Okay, but I don't want to ever come back here. I'm tired of this place."

"We'll leave and you'll never have to come here again!"

We left. It was raining. The sun was setting. "I don't want anyone to know we're leaving," I said. He covered me with a cape. The river was swollen and we couldn't cross. "We'll have to hire a raft," the *mezcal* seller said.

"But he's going to know I'm leaving with you!"

"Keep yourself covered; here he comes! Quick, get up!"

The raft man didn't recognize me. What happiness! Now
people couldn't talk about me anymore. "What ever happened to
Benita?" would be all they could say. "Have you seen her?"

We walked on. Finally we arrived at a town where no one
knew me. We had dinner. "Now what?" I asked him.

"Nothing! I will fix a bed for you and your daughter and I
promise I will leave you alone."

I slept peacefully, because I no longer had worries about food.
But I couldn't stop thinking that all this would have to be paid back
somehow. The sun came up. We started walking again. He had
about twenty mules carrying coconuts he was taking to his village.

When we arrived at a place they call Pie de la Cuesta, he said,
"Now we're almost at Acapulco. So what are you going to do with
the girl?"

"What do you mean? I'm taking her with me!"

"You can't, because we are going to my people and everyone
will know she isn't mine. Why don't you leave her with her
grandmother?"

"Why do I have to leave her with anyone?"

"Why do you want to bring her with you? We're going to be
travelling a lot and we can't bring her. We're going through
Acapulco and you can leave her with your family."

"Fine, I'll think of something."

When we got to Acapulco I made up my mind. I went to see
my mother-in-law. "I'm going to leave my daughter here for a
while," I told her.

"Yes, of course!" she said. "I love that little girl. But where
are you going?"

"I don't really know!"

"Fine, leave her here."

I left my daughter. I went back to my man. "She's with her
family," I said to him.

"Let's go; now you'll be more relaxed."

"Not at all! How could I leave the thing I love most in my
life?"

"Everything will work out in the future."

We continued our journey. We arrived at a place called La
Sabana. We got down from our horses to eat. There was a woman
there, with white hair. She took me out behind the house.

"Are you the *mezcal* seller's woman now?" she asked me.

I told her the whole story.

"Just be careful," she said. "This man recently had a young and beautiful lover. Her name was Angela. One time he came here with her. I saw how badly he treated her. He made her clean the saddle blankets of the animals like she was a servant. One time he gave her a beating and she died. So you just be very careful."

We continued walking. I was thinking about what the woman with the white hair had told me. "What are you thinking about?" the *mezcal* seller asked me. "Aren't you happy?"

"Yes, of course!"

We walked and walked. I thought and thought.

The *mezcal* seller liked to drink along the way. He got drunk. I started to feel afraid. Before we got to the next town, he sent one of the servants ahead to tell his wife not to look for him, because he had a woman with him and if she caused trouble he would whip her. I heard it all and I was thinking that my suffering was about to begin. I acted like I hadn't heard anything. By the time we got there, he was completely drunk. I was so afraid! What would this man do to me? Well, we would soon see!

It was about midnight. He ordered dinner to be prepared.

"It's ready, señor!"

"Fine, let's eat, everyone!"

After we had eaten, he said, "Now to sleep; you fix the woman's bed." One of the servants put out the cot. I laid down. Then he came over to me. "How are you? Is everything all right?"

"Yes."

"Time to sleep; someone just told me there's a gang of robbers around here and that they'll steal women, too. I have some *centavos* for him. You have to hide."

"But they steal mules, too" said one of the servants.

"That's why we can't let them wander off much and we all must be alert."

"Aren't you afraid they'll get you?" someone asked me.

"Well, let's wait and see what happens."

I slept for a while, until a shout woke me up. "Long live Rosalío Radilla!" We all stood up. Someone handed me a machete. If it's Radilla, I thought, I will kill him, because he is the assassin of my *pueblo*, he is the one who killed all the Escudero boys, those who gave land to the *campesinos* and fought against the Spaniards so they'd lower the price of corn. Then another "Who goes there!"

was heard outside, but closer now. "We come in peace," was our answer.

"What are you carrying?"

"*Mezcal.*"

"What else?"

"That's all."

"Pour us a carafe then."

They carried out the *mezcal*. The Radilla men started drinking. I was hiding behind a tree, terribly frightened. My legs were buckling under me. I heard them talking. "Where is the general?"

"He left. The Spaniards gave him a boat so he could go, because if he had stayed they would certainly kill him."

"But the government is on his side."

"Yes, but the people are angry."

"But we can fix that. We'll fuck over anyone who isn't on our general's side!"

The Radilla men walked off, drinking *mezcal*. I returned to the house. What fear I felt. Now to sleep; tomorrow I had to wake up early. We got into our beds. Soon you could hear gunshots nearby. Everyone got up again. What was going to happen? "Give me a pistol," I shouted.

"But what do you want it for, if you don't know how to shoot?"

"Give it to me, they're getting closer!"

The gunshots were getting louder: Boom! Bang! They were coming! Now the battle would begin! There were shots everywhere, and finally they came over to where we were. "You, come here," they said to the *mezcal* seller, and they took him off with them.

I watched them walk away, beating him. What could I do? If I go outside, they'll get me, too. I called the servants over. "We have to rescue him!"

"How can we?" they asked.

"Look—we'll start running behind the mules, shouting 'Viva Rosalío Radilla' the whole time so they'll think we're with them."

That's what the servants did; they started the mules running, shouting at them, "Rra, rra, rra!" The servants began running behind them. "Long live Rosalío Radilla! Let the *mezcal* seller go! Let him go!"

They made a racket. The Radilla men thought there were

many of them. "Who are you?" they asked.

"We were sent by the Spaniards."

"But why do they want us to let him go?"

"Because the Spaniards owe him a favor."

The Radilla group fell for the trick and they released him. The servants returned to the inn with him. We waited a while for the gang to leave. We were silent. Nobody said one word. They mounted their horses. For some reason no one said anything. We left about five that morning. In the village we saw some dead *campesinos*. We walked on, silent, silent.

Finally, after a long time, the *mezcal* seller said, "Damn! You know how to take a risk! I swear I couldn't believe it! Thank you for what you did to save me. Really, I don't know how it happened."

"Neither do I," I said.

"From this moment on my horse and my pistol are yours, for your use. And later, I will divorce my wife and marry you."

"You're married?"

"Yes, but my wife doesn't know how dangerous it is out on the road."

I thought a lot about what he had said. Two days later he asked me again. "I'm arranging my divorce," he said.

"Fine, I will be your wife. But who is your wife now?"

"Joaquín's sister; he's the servant who takes care of you."

The next day was the feast of the Virgin of Guadalupe. "Aren't you going to take me to the party?" I asked him.

"I can't, I have to go out and Joaquín's going with me. If you want to go, take Genaro with you."

I went with Genaro. That's when some men arrived. One of them said to me, "What's happening, what are you doing here?"

"Who are you?"

"Oh, you don't know me anymore? Don't you remember when we used to go drinking together?"

"I have no idea who you are. And I don't know what you're talking about!"

"Just come with us; we'll tell you where we met you."

They took me by the hand. The servant went off, leaving me there alone. We were already far away when I saw the *mezcal* seller coming. He caught up with us. "Friends, where are you taking her? Don't you know she's going to be my wife?"

"We didn't know, we thought she was just passing through here. And you know, we take whatever woman we like the looks of . . . "

"That's not it at all," the servant said. "Your wife paid them to take that woman away; she paid them good money."

The *mezcal* seller was furious. He grabbed me by the hand and went into the nearest bar to drink beer. He got drunk. I was with him the whole day. Then it was night. He took me off to the side. "Do you know those men?" he asked me.

"No."

"I'll kill you if you don't tell me the truth!"

"But I really don't know them!"

"I said I'll kill you if you don't tell me the truth!"

I didn't lose control. He yelled at me for a long time. He took out his pistol and held it to my chest. When he least expected it, I kicked him in the shin and snatched the pistol away from him. I took him as my prisoner and pushed him back into the house. I made him lie down. Soon he fell asleep. He stopped fighting with me.

The next day he demanded, "Give me the pistol!"

"Do you remember what you did to me last night?"

"Me?"

"Yes! Now I'm the one who will kill you. I won't give you the pistol until you tell me what you plan to do about your wife."

"What do you mean? She's going to pay for what she did. Things are going to change."

"But she has more right than I do . . . "

"No, she doesn't know what I owe you. You are my right hand. I owe you my life. I'm going to tell her so right now."

"But you told me you were already getting the divorce. I can't allow that. I'm leaving. I don't want to be here with you."

"I'll never let you leave. Look—"

"Come hell or highwater, I'm going."

"I tell you, I won't let you go."

"Okay, but promise me you won't leave your wife.

"Okay then, I won't divorce her, but you will stay with me."

MEXICO CITY AT LAST

We were on the road for six months. The *mezcal* seller had a woman in every town. I knew it all from the beginning. None of his women bothered me. He would go off with them, and I was happy. I didn't love him, so why should I get involved in things that didn't interest me? The only thing I knew was that he treated me well—I had food, I had clothes. I was the one who gave orders to the servants. I handled all the money. On the road, I made the decisions, but once we arrived at Tixtla, his wife was the one who ruled.

I knew I couldn't betray him, that I couldn't leave him after all he had done for me. And I thought about how close I was to Mexico City! How much I had wanted to go! One day I told him. "Listen, I want to go to Mexico City," I said.

"Yes, I'm going to take you. Just let me take care of some business and then we're on our way."

Time went by and nothing. One day I got sick and he had to leave me in Acapulco to get well; he said when he came back we would go to Mexico City. A few days went by and the *mezcal* seller didn't return. One day I saw a friend of mine. "What's going on, weren't you going to Mexico City?" she asked me.

"Yes, I'm just waiting to get some money so I can go."

"How much do you have now?"

"All I have is thirty *pesos*."

"What a shame; I'm leaving tomorrow and we could have gone together."

"I really wish I could go, but I just don't have enough money. What should I do? Should I go? How much does it cost to get there?"

"It all comes out to about a hundred *pesos*," she said.

"Well that's it then; there's no way."

I went back to my corner, thinking about what I should do. Well, I'll just go, I thought. I knew the *mezcal* seller was owed some money in certain towns and I could go over to Tierra Colorada and see a man who owed him about a thousand *pesos* in merchandise and I'd get money from him. Then I'd use it to go to Mexico City. After all, I had a sister there and I could work with her. I knew that until I learned how to do things, I would get lots of beatings, but so what? I wanted to see if my luck would change. I might find a rich man to live with, or at least someone I loved. I wanted to feel love, a passion that I'd never experienced. What would it be like?

I went back to my friend's house and told her my idea. "Do you think he'll pay you the money?" she asked me.

"Of course. Everyone around knows me as his wife and no one would turn me down."

"Fine, then we'll leave tomorrow."

I went to see my daughter. I kissed her. "I'm going far away, baby, but I'll be back to you. You know your mother is going, but she won't forget her daughter." I kissed her again. She started whimpering.

As I left, I was thinking, if the *mezcal* seller sees me, he'll give me such a beating I won't even be able to remember what day I was born. We hired some animals as far as the place to get the car for Iguala that goes to the train. Fine, so I went to Tierra Colorada and asked the man for the money. "Yes, of course, señora, here's your money."

"Thank you. When my husband comes to collect the money, tell him I came and asked you for it already. And tell him that I'm going to Mexico City and I'll take many memories of him with me."

"Excuse me, señora, but are you running away?"

"Of course I am!"

"Well then give me back the money!"

"I'm not giving you anything! Tell him you gave it to me. He's a good man and he won't get angry. He thinks only of me, and of how much he loves me. But in this situation I couldn't continue, just going along. I was happy because he didn't rush me into anything. I had servants. I could order them around. They obeyed my commands. I had a good horse, a pretty black one that danced beneath the reins and climbed on rocks. I am leaving the two things I love most in life—but what can one do—I'm going to try my luck!"

The poor man didn't know what to do or what to say. I took the money and said goodbye. He stood for a long time at the door, watching me go. He didn't say a word.

We caught the train . . . and finally, I was in Mexico City!

In the Struggle

THE CABARET

It was about eight o'clock at night when I arrived. I didn't have any impression: not even happiness. I felt as if I had been there before. I was thinking about so many things and so many adventures and that maybe there would be more after Mexico City . . .

I reached at my sister Lupe's house. I didn't tell her anything about my life, because I didn't feel like talking to anyone. I only thought about being good, that I would go to school to learn to read and once I had learned, I would find a job so I could go back for my daughter.

About four days after I arrived, my sister told me, "Wash the floor." My God! How am I going to do that, I thought, as big as it is, and I don't even know how it's done; you don't wash floors where I come from because the floors are made of brick, but here they're pure wood. Wash the floor! I wet the entire room and nothing got cleaner. Then my sister came home. "Well, well, you can't do this, either? You're a woman now. You have a daughter and you haven't learned anything. So what are you going to do? Don't think I'm going to support you your whole life! You're not a girl anymore. How are you going to support your daughter? You idiot, you're no good even as a servant! And you want to learn to read, too. You're really something!"

"So you think I'll never learn to read? I'll go to school at night!"

"It gets very cold here at night!"

"I don't care; I want to learn to read!"

"And if you get pneumonia?"

"Fine, then, I won't go. I'll see if someone will pay me to be a babysitter, so I can save some money and go get my daughter."

"That's a good idea, but not right now. First get to know Mexico City and then do it. Wait two months to see if you like it."

During those two months, I would go to La Lagunilla market to buy all the household things. Finally one day my sister said, "It's time for you to look for a job, Benita." The next day I went out on the street planning to look for work. I walked all the way down Allende Street. Then I went to Santiago Park. I sat there for a while. I was very tired. Then I went back home.

I had been with my sister for about five months. She was

angry because I didn't find a job, and she treated me worse and worse. She beat me so much I forgot my own name. Then I thought about going back home; I could work there, selling things, and then I could get my daughter back. But how could I get back there now? With what money?

I was desperate. I stole thirty *pesos* from my sister and went to the station, so I could use it for the train to Iguala. But since I didn't know how to read, I got on the wrong train. On the way, as we were coming to a small town, I asked a woman, "Excuse me, señora, where are we?"

"Tulancingo."

It scared me to hear that and I started to cry. "Where do you want to go?" she asked me.

"To Iguala, Guerrero."

I didn't know what to do. I kept on crying. Then the conductor of the train took an interest in my dilemma. He told me not to worry, that I should get off at Tulancingo, and he would get me back to Mexico City and my family.

I stayed in Tulancingo for a day, and then he took me to Mexico City. But I didn't want to go back to my sister's because I was scared of the whipping she would give me for stealing thirty *pesos*, so I decided to go with the conductor to a guest house. Soon he rented a house for me.

He traveled constantly, so I was almost always alone. Once he went to Tampico and stopped writing me. The time went by and he didn't come back. He's gone, I thought. Now the only thing to do is look for work.

One day a woman told me, "Benita, I'm going to pay you to pick something up for me. Do you know where Cinco de mayo Street is?"

"I think I know it well enough!"

I wasn't sure how to find the number of the house, so she told me where to go. She gave me a *tostón* so I could take a taxi. I went out into the street. A taxi went by. I called it over. I gave the driver the paper with the address. We arrived. "Here it is; it's this building," the driver said.

"Oh! But where should I go? It's enormous!"

The driver realized I wasn't from Mexico City. "If you want," he said, "I'll go with you."

"Okay."

We went to the elevator. "Get in," he said.

"I'm not getting in there!"

"Why not?"

"Who knows where it will take me?"

"But it will take you up, where you have to go."

"Well maybe so, but I'm not going."

The driver was laughing. "Okay. What is it you have to do?"

"I have to deliver this letter. If you want to, you go."

"Fine, give it to me!"

I was so afraid of the elevator . . . when he came back, I asked him where this animal had taken him. He laughed and explained what an elevator was. "Fine, now take your money," I said.

"No, señorita, really it's nothing. And I'm going to take you home, because if I don't you'll get lost. Get in the car."

"But—then it will be two *tostones* and she only gave me one."

"But I'm not going to charge you anything!"

"Okay, let's go!"

He asked me where I was from. "I'm from San Gerónimo, Guerrero," I told him.

"How nice! Tell me, is it beautiful there?"

"I don't know."

"What do you mean you don't know?"

"I don't!"

"It must be beautiful, because you are."

"Maybe, but I don't like it."

"Oh, come on!"

Every time someone asked me about my home, my heart skipped a beat. I have to go, I said to myself, thinking about my daughter, but only if things work out here first. And I'll bring her back with me.

We arrived at the house. "Do you really live here?" he asked me.

"Yes."

"Well, we'll be seeing each other again."

He was young, about eighteen years old, dark skinned with curly hair, very nice. After all, I thought, he treated me very well. He didn't even charge me for the ride. I saw him two days later. He called me over from his car. "Come on, señorita, I'll give you a ride."

"No thank you."

"Come on, I have many things to tell you."

I got in. He invited me for an ice cream. He told me his name was Manuel Rodríguez, that he really liked me, and wouldn't I like to be his girlfriend? "But listen," I said. "Since you met me you've been calling me señorita; and I'm a señora—I have a daughter!"

"No!"

"Yes, and I'm going to bring her here with me."

"What, she doesn't live with you?"

"No."

"Are you a widow?"

"No, her father left me before she was born."

"Who is she living with now?"

"With her grandmother."

"Do you get along with her grandmother?"

"Yes."

"Then, when you go to get her they won't want you to leave again."

"Who knows! Okay, I have to go. Thank you."

We parted. What a nice boy. I talked about him to some of my neighbors. "We know about those drivers," they told me. "Ever since they took my daughter away, the ones from Gray Automobiles, just look at her, the poor thing, she walks around scared to death." She told me about how the men from Gray Automobiles took a group of girls to Chapultepec park and did all kind of horrible things to them. Her daughter has been slow ever since then, but . . . I was already a little in love.

The months went by; we had relations. He would come see me, and was always good to me. Love grew between us. He promised to give me the car; he said that his father had given it to him anyway. He told me he was a student, but that he would work to give me everything he earned and that when he had money, he would go for my daughter, that he would take care of her.

"Let's go for a ride," he said one day.

"Okay, let's go."

I trusted him, like always. He took me to a hotel. What a disappointment! "You aren't going back to your house. You'll stay here with me," he told me. I couldn't convince him to take me back home so I stayed with him. He began to take me with him everywhere. I went to dances. He took me on rides around town.

Since I still didn't really love him, I would always think, it's just my luck, they always take me away with them before I love them . . .

He took me many places. He loved me too much. He took me to meet his mother, who loved me very much.

I had been living in Mexico City one year by then. Sometimes I would cry, thinking of my girl. He would say, "Just wait, as soon as you have some money you can go for her. I'm going to keep giving you money to save until you have enough to go get her."

He gave me one *tostón* every day. But months went by and I still didn't have any money saved. "This car doesn't make you any money," I told him. "Everyday you have to pay a fine; the tire, the headlight . . . " Whatever he earned he gave to his father. He said he couldn't earn much with his car because it was old. He said that he would get a new one so more people would hire him and then he'd have money and I could go for my little one. One day I sent a letter to my mother-in-law saying I would be coming for my daughter soon. The old woman answered, telling me how much it had cost her, and that if I had three thousand *pesos*, I could have my girl.

When Manuel came home he read the letter. "Soon you'll have the money for your trip and your expenses," he told me.

"But how can you do it? It's not just the money for the trip I need now."

Two years went by and he had just about all the money we needed. Then he crashed his car and had to get away from Mexico City in a hurry. I spent all the money I had saved. Two months went by and his mother heard nothing about him; neither did I. I started to feel desperate. I would cry and his mother would try to console me. "When my child comes back, he'll take you to get yours."

Four months had passed since Manuel left. I told his mother that I was going to look for a job so I could get some money to go for my daughter. "And where are you going to work?" she asked me.

"Well, I don't know. María told me that she would take me somewhere where I could earn money."

"And you're really going to do it? Don't you know María works at a cabaret? She'll take you there and you'll lose yourself and when Manuel comes back he won't want you."

"But I keep myself pure and I won't go off with anyone until he comes back."

"Don't go; I'll give you some money."

"No, I lost Manuel by trying to get more money. He was trying to help me get my daughter back, and he isn't even her father; well I have even more reason to sacrifice myself, I want to get her."

I put on a green dress and left with María. She introduced me to the owner of the cabaret *El Viejo Jalisco* that was on San Juan de Letrán Street.

What people I found there! How the beer flowed, how the men drank, and how they tipped the girls! "You haven't seen anything," María told me. "When you see the tips, you're never going to want to leave. Now pay attention: if someone offers you a drink, you say, 'I'll have anise,' and he'll give you a token worth twenty *pesos*; if you ask for beer, you earn twenty-five; if you ask for a tea and use a token for it, you get thirty for yourself . . . "

I won't drink beer, I thought to myself, I'll drink anise and punch so I can earn money as quickly as possible and leave for my daughter, because if I wait any longer soon I'll have to pay four thousand. And where else could I get the money? I started, drinking only punch. By midnight I had quite a few *pesos*, from drinking punch with men and from tips. The next day I could barely get out of bed from staying up so late. I told my mother-in-law what I had earned. "That's no good," she said. "When my son returns, what will you tell him?"

"I'll tell him I'm a good girl."

"No you won't."

"Yes, he'll believe me and know that I never loved anyone else."

After two months in the cabaret, I knew how it went: the scratched faces, the razor blades, the drunkenness, everything . . .

THE GOVERNOR

The *El Viejo Jalisco* stood to the National Theater. For a while the actors went to the cabaret every night. Among them was the play's creator, who fell in love with me. I never went out with anyone, and at five in the morning when the cabaret closed I would take a taxi straight home, so everyone thought I was a young lady. I had assured them all that I really was, so they wouldn't bother me and they'd respect me more.

The engineer begged me every night to go out with him. I refused. He was drawn by my attitude and became infatuated with me. He came every single night, and spent a lot of money. One day an argument started between the engineer and the cabaret owner. The engineer claimed I wasn't really a virgin. The cabaret owner said I was. "I bet you a thousand *pesos* Benita's not a virgin," the engineer said.

"I accept the bet," the Spaniard answered.

They put the money on the table. To find out who won, they agreed to take me to a doctor, a friend of the engineer, so he could examine me. "Benita, don't make me a loser in this," said the Spaniard, the owner of the cabaret. Finally the day came when I was to be examined to see whether I was a virgin. We went. We arrived at the doctor's office on Insurgentes Avenue, he turned out to be a good friend of mine. I winked him so he would know what to do. The engineer said, "I have a bet that this young woman isn't a virgin and I want you to examine her and give me a certificate."

"Very well," the doctor said. "You'll have the certificate tomorrow. I will examine her right now."

Naturally, he gave me a certificate stating that I was a virgin. The engineer lost the bet. I won a hundred *pesos* for it, from the Spaniard.

Since he was sure I was a virgin, the engineer begged me to marry him. He promised me things. I refused and refused. Finally, tired of his insistence and afraid he would discover the truth, I confessed one day to the Spaniard that I wasn't a virgin and that I had a daughter.

"Fucking hell! Now we're in deep shit! How did you get a certificate from that creep?" he asked me. "No, don't tell me!" Let a few days pass and then . . .

One night I went to the cabaret and said to the girls: "It finally happened . . . "

"How could you? Who was it?"

"El Pierrot."

El Pierrot was a songwriter, and a good friend of mine.

Then the engineer came in, and the girls ran to tell him. "Benita isn't a virgin anymore," they told him. "El Pierrot did it."

"No! Is it true?"

He called me over. "Is this true, Benita?"

"Yes, it's true."

"I can't believe it. And look who you chose to do it with!"

Soon El Pierrot arrived. The engineer called him over. "Friend, sing me something," he said.

After El Pierrot sang a song, the engineer said, "Now we're going to toast your victory!"

"Which victory?"

"Don't try to fool me, my friend. Benita told me all about it!"

"I don't know what you're talking about," El Pierrot said.

"Do you mean you don't remember taking me home with you the other night and robbing me of my honor?"

"Who, me?"

"It's okay, I congratulate you," the engineer said. "You got the best one in the whole place!"

The engineer left. "It's okay, Benita," El Pierrot said to me, "I went along with the joke, but . . . now make it worth my time, or leave me alone."

Another time, a state governor started coming every night to the cabaret. He kept insisting that I go out with him. I was keeping to my plan, so I didn't go. The man was mad about me. Once he arrived, I couldn't pay attention to any other client or dance with anyone. The governor made me sit with him the whole time. If he arrived and found me dancing with someone, he would start a fight with the person I was with. I was afraid of him and when he came I would hide, but he always found me.

One day he wouldn't take no for an answer. He pulled me outside, almost by force, and to get back at me, he said we wouldn't take a taxi. We went on foot. We walked for many blocks. This was lucky for me because soon we saw a policeman. I grabbed him by the arm.

"This man is bothering me," I said. "Please take him to the

police station."

The governor took out some documents and identified himself to the policeman, who didn't know what to do.

Seeing that he didn't want to take him to jail, I added, "Besides, he stole something of mine. He took my watch. Look, there it is."

And in fact, the governor had put my watch on his wrist. This perked the policeman up and we all went to the police station, after a lot of screaming and shouting. At the station I again accused him of robbing me. They gave me back my watch and the governor stayed behind, screaming. I left and went back to the cabaret.

The next night he came in, drunk, bringing a woman with him. He called to me. I had to sit with them and have a drink. The governor insisted I sit next to him and he started to embrace me and tell me he loved me. The woman with him just sat and cried.

"What's wrong?" I asked her.

We went out to eat at a restaurant. He sat me down next to him again and embraced me. He ordered more wine and soon he fell asleep.

Then I asked the woman: "Why are you crying, señora?"

"Because this man is my husband . . . and he is in love with you . . . he only brought me here so I could meet you . . . "

She began to cry harder.

"Okay, so why don't you leave him? Come join us in the cabaret and you'll find a man here to love you."

"No, I couldn't, he'd kill me!"

The governor was still sleeping. Then I had an idea: I woke the governor up. I told him I wanted to go to bed with him. I said that he should take me to a hotel. He loved the idea. His wife and I got him into a taxi and we went to a hotel. He was staggering from so much drink. We put him in bed. I acted like I was going to get in with him. I turned off the light and told his wife to lie down next to her husband. Then I left without his knowing it.

The next day he showed up, furious with me. "Oh, you little witch! You traitor! There I was, thinking I was in bed with you, and this morning when I wake up I see it's my wife . . . well you haven't heard the end of this!"

A NEW LIFE

One night I was alone in the cabaret. None of the other women had arrived. Then I saw a man behind the glass door who kept passing by and looking inside. I had the strange feeling it was my husband. In fact, it was. He called to me.

"Why are you working here?" he asked me.

"I'll explain everything later."

"Well come on, let's go!"

He grabbed me by the hand and we left. He took me to his house. "If you, who aren't even my daughter's father," I told him, "have had to hide from the police, and without even ever meeting her, well then I, as her mother, have even more reason to go work in the cabaret."

"Fine, but promise me you'll never go back there."

"Why not? I'm earning good money!"

"I promise that you'll have your daughter soon."

"Okay then, I won't go back."

One day I said to him, "Why don't you forget about the taxi? After all, you don't earn much with it. It's barely enough just to get you around."

"You're right," he said. "I'm going to look for a job, something where I earn something steady."

"That's the idea; I'll help you, too. You'll see, everything will turn out for the best."

Every day Manuel went out looking for a job. Nothing! Days went by and nothing!

"Guess what," he said one day, "someone has offered me a job, but the pay is only one *peso*."

"So go on, take it! I'll live on soup and beans, but I want you to stay out of that car."

He took the job. At first they paid him one *peso*. He worked very hard. Four months later, they were paying him three *pesos* a day. That was fine, we were doing well. Later, he earned five. Then he had a commission in addition to the five *pesos*. He started to give me money so I could save for my trip.

Once he had money, he started coming home late. He dressed very well in those days. He had suits made worth a hundred *pesos*. He bought perfume and lotions. Well, he was a handsome young man. One day I said to him, "I have enough money for my trip."

"Fine, then it's time to go; take this money, too."

I left for Acapulco. When I arrived at the house where she was staying, I told the woman, "I'm here to pick up my daughter."

"No, you're not taking a thing from here!"

"Yes, I'll bring her back soon, but give her to me!"

"Look, the girl is still very young. She needs a lot of care. Besides, she's going to be living with a man who isn't her father and she'll suffer for that. Anyway, you have to pay me for what I've spent on her . . . "

So she finally convinced me and I left without my daughter. I went back to Mexico City without her. I told Manuel what had happened to me: "Well, but at least I saw her," I told him, "and my daughter is very pretty! When I have enough money, I will go back for her."

Time went by. I asked Manuel for money again so I could save enough for my next trip. "I'll give it to you," he said, "but if you come back again without her, I'm not going to give you anymore."

So I made my plan: I would sneak into the house, and once I got there, I would find where she was playing and grab her. I would have a car waiting to take her away in and then I wouldn't have to pay any of the money they were asking for. "Well, I guess you know what you're doing," Manuel said.

"I'll be leaving soon," I answered. "I'm going to take a chance on winning everything!"

In fact, I did go for my daughter, determined not to return without her. I got to Acapulco at about seven one night. I hid and watched for signs of her. I was lucky that day; I saw her playing. I grabbed her. I threw her into the car. . . and then the shouting began. "A woman just took your daughter!"

"Who could it be?"

"Who knows!"

They sent for the police. Then they found out that her mother had grabbed her. They looked for me everywhere. I hid at the *El Quemado* ranch, which belonged to my brothers. They dug a pit in the earth and I crawled in with my daughter when the police came near. I knew the authorities were looking for me, so I didn't come out for anything. I knew that if I did I would lose her, because they had money to pay the police and, as everyone knows, money goes to those who already have some, even though it's not fair.

Later I bought myself a pistol, because, I thought: they can try to get my daughter away from me, but I'll kill them if they do. I had been hiding for five days when I suddenly realized that they knew where I was, but now, knowing what to expect, I hid in a thicket with my daughter, holding the gun in my hand. I was shocked to see the armed police coming for my daughter. All was lost. If I fired my weapon, they'd get me for sure. But I had made up my mind; I thought it would be better for them to kill me. I was so tired of the life I had to live. Wherever I looked, I was obliged to sell myself for my daughter.

The police didn't find me and I escaped after all. I went to a house and asked for shelter. The man of the house said he didn't want any trouble and he couldn't let me stay there. Then I went down to the river. I cried and cried, holding my little girl in my arms. I spent the night frightening the mosquitos away; I couldn't sleep at all. In the morning I went to another ranch. I stayed there two days and then I left for Mexico City. I arrived with my daughter.

There was a surprise waiting for me in Mexico City. My husband had gone off with a very good friend of mine, such a good friend that I invited her to my house for lunch and we spent the rest of the afternoon talking. Then Manuel's mother said to me, "You see? It's your fault; why did you go away?" I went to look for Manuel. I found him at his job. "What's going on with her?" I asked.

"It's nothing," he said. "I'm going to keep giving you money, because after all I owe you my life; to you and only you. You can stay in my house, with my mother, and you will have everything you need."

Time went by. Then I got desperate, and I went back to the cabaret. I arrived there one night. I found the friends that I had left behind with their faces cut up. Another was in jail, for robbery. I thought that if I went back there the same thing would happen to me, but I wasn't going to be foolish about it, I would behave well in order to avoid the suffering that the other women had to endure.

Soon they said that all the cabaret women had to get a health certificate. And I thought I should get one because now I had someone to support, who was my responsibility. The day that the Health Department had given for the women to get their cards arrived. I told my mother-in-law about it. "Why do you want one?"

she asked me. "After all, my son will take care of you!"

"Yes, but I don't like the way that another woman has taken my husband away from me."

"So why don't you take back what belongs to you from that woman?"

"I already have what belongs to me, my daughter."

"You're afraid of this woman who stole your husband."

"No, it's not that; but I would end up in jail and if I go to jail I want it to be for a good reason."

"You should get him back from that woman. After all, you helped him to become a man, and this is how he repays you . . . "

"Well, I'd rather get my health card than go looking for him."

"Fine, but don't come crying to me later!"

I got my card and stayed at the cabaret for five months. I had men in love with me who offered me beautiful houses and all, but I was afraid, and I didn't want any more problems. I kept myself pure, living just from the tips I got. There were nights I earned up to five *pesos*, depending on the customers.

One day I was sleeping when Manuel came over. "I know you've been working at the cabaret," he told me. "A friend of mine told me. You're shameful!"

"So what, I'm happy, I earn money."

"Yes, but I don't like it; I don't want you in places like that. Look, I'm coming back to you. That friend of yours took everything I had: my watch, my money, and it made me realize that my woman was the only one for me and I hope you'll be happy now. So are you going to stop going to those dens of iniquity?"

"Okay, I'll stay here with you."

"Of course you will. Now on to a new life!"

BENCHO THE GOAT

We found a house in a neighborhood near José Joaquín Herrera Street. It was a terrible area. There were seventy houses, all without bathrooms, and with two toilets and ten sinks for all the tenants. The rent was sixteen *pesos*. Every morning the neighbors fought about the sinks. The first ones to get there got to do their wash. As they shook out their clothing the water spattered all over. "Hey, you're getting me wet! Stop throwing your filth all over. . ."

"Well if ya don't like it, why doncha go live in the Lomas de Chapultepec? They got some real beautiful houses there."

The kind of clothing the neighbors washed was used as a way to classify them. My clothes were a little better than the others, so they called me "the queen of the courtyard." There were some others like me. We organized ourselves, the queens against the rest, against the poor ones, so we could defend ourselves. In the conversations at the sinks all the women chattered about the lives of their neighbors. "Did you know Natalia's husband is living with another woman and he only comes around now and then to see her; and the shameless thing lets him in, as if it were no big deal!"

"But she's right," said another one, "when she says she has no one else to support her. All she can do is try to put up with it."

There was a woman named Juanita; she was married to a huge man who worked on the railway. Every morning they bought a twelve liter cask of *pulque* liquor and took it home. Then about noon, all you could hear were the beatings and the screaming. Who would win this time? We all hung around the door, to see who would come out first. Time went by and neither of them appeared. The two of them must have knocked each other out. Later that night Juanita came out, with her face wrapped up in a *rebozo* or in a towel. "What happened, Juanita?" someone would ask.

"Nothing, nothing, I've just been a little sick. I had a   fever . . ."

She would never betray her husband. And the beatings went on every day.

In the house next to me there were some spiritualists, and each night they would practice very strange things. At midnight they would walk around their little balcony with lit candles and some wax dolls. "Benita," people would say to me, "beware of your neighbors, don't let them put a spell on you."

One Sunday, Manuel took me out for a car ride to Contreras.
On the way back, a newborn baby goat crossed the road in front of
us. I got out of the car and stole it for myself. It was beautiful. My
father used to have a pretty little nanny goat. Her name was Bencha.
So I called the baby he-goat Bencho. I loved him. I kept him in my
room and took him out to play on the patio with the children in the
neighborhood. But a few months went by and Bencho grew big and
became very aggressive. He would jump the fence and run away.
In time, he started to grow horns and loved to butt into people.

The neighborhood children had made him fierce. One time
when I wasn't home, the goat ran off and went into the spiritualists'
house. He knocked over the flowerpots and chewed their pillows
and bedspread. When I got home I didn't see Bencho in the house.
I went out to look for him. The spiritualists had him locked up and
they were hitting him. I took him away from them. But from that
moment on, we were enemies. Every time we saw each other we
would shout and yell threats. I told Manuel what had happened, and
that every day our neighbors provoked me. "If I come home one
day and see you bickering with those old women," he said, "don't
think I'm going to defend you—you'll get a beating from me
instead. If they continue to insult you, it's your fight, and I find you
beat up, I'll hit you, too . . . so don't go around making a scandal."

I kept fighting with the spiritualists, but one day a woman
named Isabel said to them, "Don't even dirty your hands with her;
leave it to me." I was very angry. I went into the house and grabbed
the first thing I saw, which was a fork. I went outside and attacked
her with it. I stabbed her in the ribs. The fork stuck inside her. Then
the real uproar began. The police came and took me to the station.
Soon Manuel came; he paid the twelve *peso* fine that they had
charged me and we left. We hadn't even turned the corner when
Manuel gave me such a thrashing that it left me on the ground. He
hit me so hard the hair stood up on my face and he left the imprint
of his fingers on my cheek.

The police commissioner saw this and ordered Manuel arrested. They ran up to us. "Señora, what is going on?"

"Nothing!"

"What do you mean nothing, what's that I see on your face,
eh?"

They threw Manuel in jail. I went to see the police commissioner, to beg him to let my husband free, pleading that he hadn't done anything wrong. The commissioner refused. I begged and pleaded him. I wouldn't leave; I stayed there, insisting. This happened at four in the afternoon. At four in the morning, they finally freed him to my care. We left. We fought the whole way home. We had walked about two blocks when he grabbed me again, slapping me. He threw me down and then grabbed me by the hair and dragged me along the street.

As for my poor Bencho . . . I had to give him away.

THE EIGHT HOUR DAY

One day Manuel showed up with a pile of advertisements that he and someone else were going to paste up on walls. "What does all that paper say?" I asked him.

"Don't you know I've joined the Communist Party?"

"So what's that?"

"It's the party of the workers; a party that defends our rights, just like the one they have in Russia. Their main concern is the workers and that's why I joined up with them. The comrades will be here soon and we're going to hand all this paper out, because tomorrow is May 1st."

"So what is May 1st?"

"It's the anniversary of the Chicago killings, when the workers in the United States started their fight for the eight hour day, and also some other things, but it's too much to explain right now. I'll tell you about it later. If I don't come home tonight it's because I've been arrested. My woman will take good care of herself, right?"

"I want to go with you."

"No, not this time; there will be other days."

He left the house. He didn't come home that night. It was morning and nothing! He must be in jail, I thought. And what would become of me now? With no husband and a daughter to support. Back to the cabaret? I went out to look for him. I asked the guard at police headquarters whether Manuel Rodríguez was jailed there. "Yes," he answered. "They arrested him last night for offending the Prime Magistrate."

"Who's that?"

"What do you mean, who is that! It's the President of the Republic. All those who offend him and who have ideas like the man you're looking for, will end up in jail."

He frightened me. This was going to be difficult, I thought. "Excuse me, señor, but what can I do to get him out?"

"Nothing, señora. No one can do anything for someone who has insulted the President!"

I left, crying. What could I do? Nothing! The man told me there was nothing I could do. I went home. Soon a man from the Communist Party came to the house. "Señora, in the name of the

Communist Party of Mexico I bring you greetings of solidarity for what has happened to your husband . . . "

"Oh! Then it's your fault he's in prison? We'll just see what I do about this!"

I felt like hitting him. I insulted him, I screamed and yelled, I said many things to him, I told him to get out of the house, but he sat through it all. "Señora," he said, "please calm down! We need your help to get Manuel out of jail. You must help us."

"But how, if the police told me there was nothing I could do?"

"Come with us to a meeting and talk to the people."

"And what do I say to them?"

"Tell them your husband is in prison for telling the truth and for defending the workers."

We went to the meeting. On the way they explained what the Communist Party was that Manuel was fighting for, and why he had been arrested, and why we had to talk to the people and what we had to say. We arrived at the Hidalgo Plaza. That was where we had our meeting. Some other speakers went first and then it was my turn. I don't even know what I said. It was the first time I ever spoke in public. While I was talking, the police came and the problems started. They took me to jail; they said it was for disrupting the public order.

They put me in prison. And now what would I do?—I said to myself. My husband in jail. Me, a prisoner, and my daughter? What would happen to her? They took my statement at headquarters. "Why did they arrest you?" they asked me.

"I don't know!"

"You don't know? Fine, then you'll be jailed for ignorance!"

Seeing the injustice of it, I started thinking that my husband must also be in jail for a just cause and that I should follow him in his path: to fight for others, for the poor, for the oppressed, as my husband would say. And since I had led a miserable life, and I knew what poverty and hunger were, I understood that the only route was the workers' way.

About five days later they set me free for lack of evidence, but my husband was still being held. I continued to fight with all my heart to get him free. But Manuel stayed in jail. They planned another meeting in Santa Julia Plaza. I went there and spoke again, protesting my husband's being in jail, and also Japan's aggression against China. The Party comrades had explained some things to me.

The police came, and . . . back to jail!

I wondered why they arrested me. All I had done was to protest about my husband and ask them to end the war between China and Japan because it was unjust. I protested because the imperialists sent oil to Japan so it can continue its war against China. Is that just?

I became interested in things like these and to ask the comrades to explain what I still didn't understand: about imperialism, and Japan, and China, and everything else.

A few days later I was free again. But not my husband. They told me to go see the Judge at the Court of First Instance. I went and he received me in his office. I told him I wanted my husband to be set free. He told me he was acting on orders of President Ortíz Rubio, and that only by Ortíz's order could my husband go free. But as it was not possible to see him . . .

Then I got some kids together. I told them to say I was their mother and Manuel their father. My trick got some results; I was finally able to get my husband out of jail, after a month.

The judge ordered his release at about ten one night; by the time I got to the penitentiary it was eleven. Since it was late, they didn't want to release the prisoner. Finally, after much whimpering, they set him free. We left together. On the way home he promised he would never forget it, that I would always be his wonderful woman; he went on and on.

We were happy again. Now he explained to me all the things I did not yet understand. "What is that about the eight hour day?" I asked him.

"That means that no one should have to work more than eight hours a day."

"And capitalism, what's that? And what does bourgeoisie mean?"

He explained it all to me and I started to understand, although not very well. I listened to his explanations but sometimes I didn't understand them. He continued his work with enthusiasm. One night he called me over. "Benita, I have to go out soon; sew this button on for me."

"I won't do it!"

"What??"

"That's right! I've already worked my eight hours and you

told me no one should have to work more than eight hours a day . . . "

He laughed and held me to him. "You're wonderful," he said.

But a few weeks later, he fell in love with another woman and left me. So I was on my own again, with my daughter . . .

THE ACCUSED

While I was living with Manuel, Jorge Pino Sandoval would often visit us. He was very young then, and belonged to the Communist Party. In those days he was fighting as a revolutionary. He had not yet betrayed the worker's cause. Since he was so broke, he was almost always at our house, because I fed him. He always came over, asking for a loan or some other favor. Those penniless Communists bored me; they only came to coax something out of Manuel and so that I would feed them. Pino tried to explain to me why the Communists never had any money, and why they never had anything to eat. He talked about their difficult struggle in those days against the Calles regime that persecuted the workers, and about the Communist Party, who were the vanguard of the fight against the Calles policies, the proletariat, on the front line confronting Calles. He told me about the war between the classes . . .

"War between the classes, my foot," I would say to him. "The truth is the Communists are a bunch of lazybones who don't want to work!"

"That's not true, Benita. Listen, let me explain it to you."

I teased him because I liked to hear his explanations. But when Manuel arrived, Pino would put aside his political explanations.

"Are we going to eat now, Benita?" he would say. "Manuel's home. Aren't you hungry, Manuel?" The three of us would eat together. Then he would ask me for a loan and he would leave. The next day and every day he would be there. One day I decided to not give him anything to eat, to see whether he would leave. I had prepared a very delicious chicken *mole*. When I heard Pino coming, I ran to the kitchen and covered the pots. Pino came in. "Hi, Benita!" he said in his high-pitched voice. "It smells great in here!" It was the chicken *mole*.

"Yes," I said, "we just ate chicken *mole*. It smelled wonderful, but the aroma is all that's left."

"What! You didn't eat already!"

"Well, yes we did. You were late today."

"How could you, Benita!"

Just then Manuel came home. "Give me something to eat,

Benita, I'm starving!"

"So you haven't eaten yet!" Pino said. "Great!"

I acted like it was all a joke. Damn it, I thought to myself, so much for that. Pino rubbed his hands together in delight. But after that, whenever he came to the house, he would go directly to the kitchen and look into the cooking the pots.

"Excuse me, Benita," he would say, "What are we going to eat today?"

By then I had joined the Communist Party, and that's why it didn't affect me much when Manuel left me. I knew that the best thing for me was to stay in the revolutionary movement. I dedicated myself fully to the struggle. I prepared myself, asking the comrades about whatever I didn't understand, listening to the Party speakers at the meetings. The police knew me very well, and because I was always at the meetings, I was one of the first ones to be arrested.

One night, a group of Trotskyites came over; they were friends of my husband. I was going out to paste up flyers that night, inviting people to a demonstration commemorating the death of Julio Antonio Mella. "Hey, what's up?" I asked them. "Does anyone want to come post flyers with me?"

"Great! Let's go!" they said. "But what if we get caught?"

"Oh, who cares about that!"

"Okay, let's go." I said, "I'll paste up the flyers and you all keep watch."

We left the house. We went down Pedro Moreno Street. Soon one of the boys walked up to me. "I think there's someone following you," he said. I started walking faster. The man behind me did too. I moved faster, and then the man started running until he finally caught up with me.

"Señorita, can you give me one of those flyers you're pasting up?"

"I can't; I have to put them up on the wall," I answered.

"Come on, I just want one, don't be afraid."

"I said I can't, they have to go on the wall. Stop bothering me."

"Look, if you don't give me one, I'll have to take it away from you myself."

So I gave him one, to put him off and also to see what he would do with it.

"Fine, take it!"

"Very good, but I don't want just one, I want all of them!"

"And who are you that I should give you all my flyers?"

I continued walking, looking for a chance to run. He didn't let me get very far. He grabbed me by the arm when I reached the doorway of a store.

"You'll give me the propaganda or I'll arrest you!"

Oh, you son of a bitch, I thought, why don't you stop screwing with me!

To see if I could escape, I started screaming and yelling at the policeman. He was shouting for me to give him the flyers, and I was yelling that I wouldn't. People had started to gather around. It was nine o'clock at night. We were both screaming. "Give me that propaganda!"

"I won't!"

"Oh yes, you will . . . "

A crowd had gathered to watch us fight. "Look," I said to him, "you're not going to get a thing from me; you've brought out the Galeana in me now!"

"And what do you mean by that?"

"I mean that I said no, and I mean no, young man! Arrest me if you want, but you can't have my flyers!"

He was pulling at the papers, but he couldn't get them away from me. I thought of the bucket of *atole*, a thick corn liquid that I was using as paste; it suddenly occurred to me to throw the whole thing at him. No sooner said than done. He was bathed in it. As he was wiping his eyes, I pasted the flyers all over his body. "Son of a bitch, you've ruined my suit!" the policeman said. He was furious. "Look at that! She threw *atole* all over him!" the people were saying, "And he's a policeman!"

And that policeman was Sotomayor, the Communists' worst enemy. I tried to run away, but he caught up with me, pistol in hand. I stopped. When he came up close to me I kicked him in the shin as hard as I could and snatched the pistol away. Now I was armed, and I climbed onto the counter of a store owned by a Spaniard and I began a speech to the people gathered there. They were happy because I had disarmed a policeman.

Pointing the pistol in my hand at Sotomayor, I talked about the death of Julio Antonio Mella, about the government of Portes Gil, enemy of the workers, and accomplice in the death of our Cuban comrade Mella. I used all the Party slogans. "One move and I'll kill you," I said to Sotomayor.

I kept on talking, never taking my eyes off him. The Spaniard in the store was also furious. He hit my legs with a stick to try to get me down off the counter. I turned around now and pointed the pistol at him. "Stop fucking with me, you Spanish son of a bitch!" I said. Sotomayor was steaming mad. "Get down!" he screamed. "Get down!" But I continued, criticizing the bourgeoisie and Portes Gil. I got down from the counter when I finished my speech. "Give me the pistol," Sotomayor said. "If you give it to me, I won't arrest you."

"Do you mean it?"

"I promise!"

I recalled my village, where the winner returns the weapon to the loser and they remain friends. "Okay, you can have it."

"Come over here."

I had barely given him the gun when he kicked me in the ribs. "You are under arrest!" he said.

"You traitor! So you want to play dirty, huh?"

He took me down to headquarters. "I have someone here who was pasting up illegal propaganda," he told them, "but first I want her to pay for my suit; it cost me two hundred *pesos*."

"Well I'm going to jail," I said, "let someone else pay for the suit!"

"You have to pay for it!"

"Oh yeah? You'll barely be able to cover yourself with what I'm going to give you!"

After three days in isolation, they took me to see Belén, the police chief. "What is your name?" he asked me.

"Well the truth is, I don't know. When they arrested me, I even forgot my own name."

"Listen, you, we're not here to play. Tell me your name!"

"Fine. It's Benita Galeana."

"Mother's name?"

"I didn't have a mother."

"What??"

"That's right—no mother!"

"Your father?"

"A father, yes; if you can call him that!"

They were really mad by then. Finally they took me to my cell. That's when the shouting started. "Oh look, the lion's had cubs!" "There goes a new one!" "Bath! Send her to the baths!" And things like that. The female prisoners were all over me. "Hey, what's going on? What do you have?"

"Nothing! Just some dirt; I want to take a bath."

"Jesus! Now we've seen everything. This one isn't afraid of the baths."

"So what are you in for?" the warden asked me.

"Because I'm a Communist."

"Poor Communists, they really suffer. They're the real victims . . . but they also fight too much, and cause trouble. A few of them just left. They were a real pain! They expect to be waited on as if they were kings! I hope you aren't going to be like that too!"

"The new one's bed!" someone shouted.

"Go to your dormitory," the warden said.

The other prisoners started watching me real close. "It's another Communist," they said. "Stay away from her." No one talked to me. Five days passed.

"Benita Galeana, go to the fence! Your statement for Cordovanes!"

Ten soldiers pulled me up to my feet. Because he was so pissed off at me for taking his gun, Sontomayor became my worst enemy and tried to push me around. He tried to get me put away for a year. But I put up a good defense and he was left looking stupid. They also gave me a two thousand *peso* fine. I didn't have any money, and neither did my Party, so I was stuck in jail. I went to see the lawyer Carlos Zapata Vela and told him him how much they wanted. He promised to give it to me.

Days in prison went by. They took me out again for a statement. I saw propaganda on the street demanding the liberty of comrade Benita Galeana. I went to the office and asked the judge to let me out for two hours. "For what purpose?" he asked me.

"There's going to be a meeting and I want to be there. As soon as it's over, I'll come back to jail. I give you my word as a Communist."

"Young lady, have you no fear of the God's wrath! You are in jail for that very reason, and still you want to go to meetings!"

"Yes, sir, because that's the only way we workers can get ahead!"

"Well the answer is no!" he said. "Absolutely not!"

Fine, I thought, then I'll have to escape when the guards aren't looking.

Just then Zapata Vela arrived and paid my fine. They let me go, but first they read me their document. "I suppose you're not going to sign it," the judge said.

"If I like the sound of it, I'll sign it all right!"

He started reading. I heard him say, " The accused declares . . . "

"Damn!" I interrupted. "I knew it! I knew I wasn't guilty!"

"Why do you say that?"

"Well you just said so!"

"Where?"

"There where you said that about 'the accused . . . ' you didn't say guilty, right?"

Everyone started laughing for some reason. They were all talking about my defense. "Now sign it!" the judge said.

"Of course! Just hand me the paper!"

I started spelling out my name, putting one letter here, another there. The judge realized I couldn't read or write, but still my defense had been a good one.

"Señora," he said as I was leaving, "I congratulate you; you have a way with words. If I had known you couldn't read or write, I would have left you inside a little longer!"

"Okay, well good-bye for now! I have to hurry because there's a meeting. I hope the police leave me alone this time."

"Good-bye!" he said. "Good luck!"

The meeting had already started when I got there. I asked to speak. I had barely begun talking when a policeman came up to me. "Under arrest!" he said.

"Jesus, I haven't even started yet! Not again!"

But they arrested all the Communists, not just me. There were about twenty "Julia" wagons to take us to jail. We started a riot. We put up a fight, but they got us all.

We kept it up when we got to the prison. "F... your mother, Sotomayor!" one of the female prisoners shouted.

"That must have been Benita," he said. He walked over to us. "Was that you shouting, Benita?" he asked me.

"Me? I wouldn't bother! First of all, I don't use that kind of language . . . and anyway, I couldn't talk about your mother that way."

"Why not? I wouldn't put anything past you!"

"Because you don't have a mother, you bastard!"

Sotomayor was furious and started screaming insults at us. We answered them all. The other prisoners, hearing the shouts, took our side to protest against police violence. The whole jail got in on it. The wardens couldn't shut us up. They called in the firemen, who came with their hoses and doused us with cold water and beat us. Then we went to bed. It was a good day!

Then they took us to Peredo. They put all the Communists together and since there wasn't any food, the head of the jail sent for some bread which he paid for himself. He didn't buy enough and had to break the bread into halves. When it arrived, everyone started to scream.

"We demand a complete meal; if not, we won't eat. We declare a hunger strike!" The chief told headquarters that the Communists were getting out of line, and they sent another "Julia" wagon. They took us to the federal penitentiary.

When we got to our cells, we talked about how they would try to get us to do prison chores. We agreed not to do them. The next day, at five o'clock in the morning, we heard the sounds of the big door handles turning; they were coming to clean the prison. We woke up. "We'll grab the police by force," we all agreed, " before they start their work." The other prisoners were shouting, "Out with the Communists!" We left our cells. "Get your brooms for the chores," the prison workers told us.

"Girls!" I shouted. "Listen up! No one is to do the chores."

"You bet we won't!"

"What do you mean?" they said. "You aren't here to do what you want; you're not in your own homes, now, ladies."

"We, the Communists, are not subject anyone's wishes," we answered. "You'd best understand that and treat us well."

Then the other female prisoners started in. "Get going, girls, because if you don't, you'll get the taste of our knives!"

Seeing that the other female prisoners were against us, we decided to improvise a meeting to explain the situation to them. The women were quiet while we were speaking, and then they started to take our side. When we had finished the meeting, the women said, "We are with the Communists; we're not going to do the chores, either."

Then the Director of the Pen separated us so the riot would quiet down. They isolated the wildest ones. One to a cell; we had no contact with the others. But we made friends with the workers there and managed to communicate with each other. I was feeling as at home in jail as in my own house!

FIVE NAKED WOMEN!

At that time Alberto Gallegos, who had murdered Señora Chinta Aznar, was also in the jail. They said they were taking him to Isla Marías, but there was a rumor that they were going kill him on the way. They also said that the Communists would be taken on the same train. "Well, girls," we said to each other, "What can we do about it? Nothing, just be strong, like good Communists!"

They told us we would be leaving soon. We started shouting, calling for the overthrow of the Portes Gil government. We sang "The International", "The Varsovianka", and other revolutionary songs we knew. It raised our spirits, and at the same time impressed the others, who saw that even when faced with the Islas Marías, we Communists would sing and not cry. But we women didn't stop thinking about our loved ones. I thought about my daughter. What would become of her if they took me away?

While we were singing, a woman approached us. It was Eva Marinez, who was in prison for killing a doctor who had betrayed her and done some terrible things. "Are you all Communists?" she asked us.

"Yes, why?"

"I know some Communists: Gómez Lorenzo, Revueltas . . . they're very good men. I admire you for your selflessness, for your courage."

We became friends. "Have you eaten?" she asked us.

"No," we said.

"Well, I'll send for some food for you."

She had a servant, because she was in a cell for important people. She also had things to eat: chorizo, canned food, things like that. "As long as I'm here," she told us, "you will have everything you need!" But a few days later, when they saw her helping us and realized that she was in solidarity with us, they began treating her badly. They took away her servant, but she continued preparing meals and giving some to us. She was very good to us.

They kept saying that the boat was leaving soon for Islas Marías and that we Communists would be sent on it. We called a meeting to decide what to do. We argued about the situation. To give ourselves enough time for our comrades to think of how to help us, I proposed that when they came to take us away, we take off all our clothes and cause a scandal. I thought they wouldn't dare take us anywhere if we were naked.

The other comrades didn't like the idea. There were five of us women. I insisted that it was the only solution, because they wouldn't take us out on the street naked and if they did, it would cause a huge uproar in the newspapers and with anyone who saw us.

One afternoon a new prisoner, a "baldy," escaped from his cell; he ran off to see a female prisoner in the Women's Section with whom he was in love. The wardens were conducting a search for him from cell to cell, because they didn't know which woman he was with. The big iron doors groaned and there was a great uproar in the jail. We thought all the noise was from them getting the women ready to go to Islas Marías. We panicked. "Now you see; it's our only chance!" I told them. I quickly took off all my clothes. The other women didn't know what to do, but seeing how determined I was, they took their clothes off, too. Soon we were completely naked in our cell, waiting for them to come for us.

"A prisoner's escaped," the wardens told us, "where is he?" The iron bars of the cells groaned. We were ready, on our feet in front of the door, holding hands, and completely nude. Then the wardens came. They opened the door and walked in. When they got a look at us, they were completely shocked. "What are you all doing without your clothes on?"

"Nothing! We're waiting for you to come get us and take us to Islas Marías! We're ready! Let's go!"

"Islas Marías my ass! A prisoner has escaped and we're looking for him. And with all of you here naked, this is where he must be."

"There's no prisoner here!" we said, angry because we had taken our clothes off for nothing. The wardens searched the cell and left. We quickly got dressed.

"You see how my tactic got results?" I said to the other women. "We scared the wardens, and we're only women! Just think if we had been men!"

The days went by, and there was no word about the boat. More and more comrades were put in jail, including some who had been working to try to get us out. We lost all hope that we would be released.

One day a prison tyrant came to our cell. "By order of the

President of the Republic, all Communists are free to go," he said. We lined up and he read us the telegram. "Now," he said, you must send a message to the President, thanking him for his generosity."

"We're not sending him a thing! We're not going to thank someone who jails workers and kills peasants!"

"Then you'll stay in prison for not knowing how to respond to the President's kindness."

We began screaming and shouting: "We will stay until the workers go out onto the street demanding our freedom, until the workers in the factories denounce this government that has sold itself out to the capitalists, until the workers oblige them to let us out."

The prison tyrants just shook their heads."These Communists are the most scandalous bunch we've ever known," they said.

"Exactly! Because we know our rights!"

"Fine, then, back to your cells!"

Prisoners once more. About two hours later they returned. "All female Communists, you're free to go!" they said. We were thrilled, because we had made them understand that we, the Communists, didn't need anything, and that we weren't going to ask any favors from the President, who murdered the workers for anything. We proved that we knew how to command respect and to defend our rights anywhere in the world.

WITH THE SOLDIERS

Back out on the street, I knew my rent was due and that my landlord was very tough; he would beat me if I didn't pay the rent and might throw me out. And sure enough, he came over right away.

"The rent, señora," he said. I stayed quiet, wondering how I'd get out of it this time. "I saw your picture in the newspaper," he demanded.

"So what?" I answered.

"No, no, nothing. All I want is the rent; I don't care about anything else."

"Well, you'll have to wait a little while for it."

"No, I'm afraid I can't."

"But, what can I do?"

"You can leave or I can throw you out."

"When do I have to be out?"

"As soon as possible. Well, first the notary has to come, so I'll let him be the one to toss you out."

No money, no work, no house, I said to myself. And then this shameless old man, why does he treat me like this? That is why I fight, and will continue fighting, so that the workers realize that the rich are our enemies and that they own everything, even our freedom.

A few days went by and the notary came. He told me I was to be evicted. They gave me two months to get out. Now I had to find a job. I went out to look for work every day. Nothing! I lived in the Colonia Obrera. It was the rainy season. I would leave the house with water around my ankles, because the streets were always so muddy. When I got downtown, I couldn't even walk; my shoes were filled with mud and I was weak from not eating breakfast. I thought I would double over . . .

One day someone told me that in an ad in the newspaper they were looking for a worker over at the army barracks. I fixed myself up and went to see whether I could get the job. I walked up to the cashier. "Señor," I said, "I want to work."

"Christ, no! You're too skinny. I need someone strong."

"Let me try," I answered. "If I don't do a good job after four days, I'll quit."

"All right, come back tomorrow."

I left feeling happy. I went home and asked the doorkeeper whether he knew where my daughter was. "She went to school," he said. My poor daughter, I thought, she left without breakfast! But soon I would have money and we would eat well. I am going to show that cashier that I might be skinny but I could do a good job.

The next day I went to work. "Here I am," I said.

"Fine, let's get to work. The first task is to prepare six barrels of *agua fresca*."

Now what? I thought; I don't know how it's made. "Señor," I asked him, "how do you make *agua fresca*?"

"I will show you how to prepare all the drinks, the ices and anything else you don't know. Then you'll do it on your own."

Everything went well. The days went by. Once he asked me if I thought he should put in a restaurant. "I could sell beer," he said, "and all the soldiers would eat here. I'd accept payment on credit; they would owe me until they were paid. And since I'm the one who pays them, I myself would take the money they owed me out of their pay."

"If you did it that way," I said, "the business is a sure success."

He put in the restaurant. Since the soldiers were quartered, of course they ate there! When they were paid, they were already behind with the cashier and never had any money left over. "You see what good business we're doing?" the cashier said one day.

"Yes," I told him, "but you're exploiting the soldiers."

"How?"

"Well, don't you take all the beer they drink out of their pay?"

Another day he said: "I want you to be my companion. That way you would care for the business as if it were your own. You would pay more attention to things. Don't you think so? What do you say?"

This made me very angry. "The only thing I can say," I told him, "is this: you want me to be your woman so you can exploit me even more, so you wouldn't have to pay me a salary. That way you would have your woman and your employee at the same time. You want to exploit me just like you do the soldiers ... "

"How dare you say such things?"

And that was that. He didn't say anything more about it. I continued working there. I started to fatten up. I soon weighed 132 pounds. When I started working there I had weighed only ninety-nine. I looked good. The delivery men started flirting with me. The cashier realized that other men were paying attention to me. "If you get involved with anyone, I'll fire you."

"Don't worry," I answered, "of all those men who are in love with me, not one of them fills my heart. I want to love a man I can admire, a man who I love for real, because until now I have never really loved anyone. One day I will have a love that makes me happy. I believe that my true love hasn't even been born yet . . . "

"That's fine, but you heard what I said."

"I know what you said; just don't try anything with me. Your problem is you're jealous for nothing, because I don't love you."

He was still angry with me, so one day he asked me why I hadn't checked a card, the ones they give the soldiers. I told him that I forgot. He answered that if I wasn't more careful, he would fire me, and since he said this in front of the soldiers, they tried to encourage me. "Don't worry, sister, if he fires you, we'll quit eating here."

One day he suddenly tried to kiss me; he became angry when I refused. "You're fired!"

"That's fine; pay me what you owe me!"

"Here, take it!"

He gave me five *pesos* and sent me out on the street just because I wouldn't let him kiss me.

The soldiers found out what was going on. They told me they would boycott him until he hired me back. Thank you, that's great," I said to them. And I left, grateful for how they were helping me.

By the afternoon he had another worker, but the soldiers would not eat dinner there, or breakfast, or lunch. The food that should have been sold during those days was spoiled. He didn't sell anything, and since his business was to do business, he had to take me back. "You're back, sister?" the soldiers said when they saw me. "You see how we got results?"

"Thank you, thank you so much," I told them.

I kept trying to get on their good side. "I want to talk to you about something," I said to them one day. "I want us to have a meeting."

"What about?"

"To talk about you organizing yourselves. You know they're starting to talk about obligatory military service; you can't let that happen . . . "

"Fine; where will we have the meeting?"

"I'll tell you later, for now I just want you to arrange to be ready when I call you."

We began to meet. I told them how they should organize themselves to defend their rights. I talked about the obligatory military service that the government was planning. Time went by. I had a group of soldiers who wanted to join the Communist Party. They agreed to become a part of the cell that I was forming. Then one of the soldiers told the general about it.

One day the general came to ask me what it was all about. "It's nothing," I said.

"What do you mean, nothing?"

"Well of course I'm not going to tell you anything, because then you'll arrest me, and the soldiers, too. But I promise you there's nothing going on with the others."

"Nothing?"

"Nothing!"

"Fine, I'll trust you, but just remember that if I hear anything more about it, I'll have to arrest you."

Poor thing, I thought, he thinks he can scare me by talking about prison. I was cured of that a long time ago! Then he left.

We kept things quiet for a while, without talking or having any more meetings. One Sunday, I heard someone whistling "The International". I went to see who it was. It was some Communists who had been arrested; they didn't know I worked at the barracks. I was excited to see comrades there in the place where I worked. I went out looking for a soldier. "Who are those people making such a ruckus?"

"They're Communists who were just arrested."

"Poor boys, why do they want to be Communists?"

"They're fools, because the Calles government won't let them live long. They say they're going to kill them all."

"Poor things! What can we do to help them?"

"Nothing; they're in isolation."

"It doesn't matter; we have to do something. We have to save them!"

"But how?"

"You should go to the newspapers and tell them there are Communists in prison here."

"Well, if you want us to, we'll do it."

"And do it soon; go to the press, and tell them that there are Communists here in this prison."

The soldiers left. I couldn't contact the comrades. I knew that if I went to see them, I would be arrested, too. One soldier went to tell the newspapers. That afternoon, the dailies said that there were one hundred Communists in jail for trying to kill the Head Magistrate. This wasn't true; they had been arrested for fighting obligatory military service.

They took the Communists away that same afternoon. I didn't know where they went. "Where did they take the Communists?" I asked a soldier.

"I think they're going to take them to Islas Marias."

"Yeah? But right now, where are they right now?"

"I don't know."

"Well try to find out and let me know."

"Why do you care?"

"I'll tell you later; right now I want to know where they took them."

"Well; I'll ask around."

Soon I found out they had been taken to the National Palace. Well, I thought, I'll go look for them after work. But then it was five in the morning and I was still working; it was the day the soldiers always got drunk and bought the most beer, so I couldn't leave. I wanted to let the Party know where our comrades were. I couldn't sleep that night, thinking that the comrades would be taken to Islas Marias and the Party would not know where they were.

This is what I was imagining, but in those days the Party was more careful about members who went to jail than they are now. The Party had guards everywhere that people there could be taken prisoner. When a comrade was arrested, they followed him all the way to headquarters and put guards at all the prisons. The one who was arrested and taken in the "Julia" had to sing "The International" so that those who were watching the prisons would realize who was being arrested.

The next day I went to see the comrades. "Did you hear about the comrades who were arrested yesterday?" I asked them.

"We already know about it. Now we must go to the factory workers and call some meetings to protest their arrest. Go see José Revueltas and see if you can plan something to try to save our comrades."

I went to look for Revueltas. The police had orders to arrest me again. Then I found him. "Sister, I've been looking for you, we have to organize a meeting for the prisoners," he said.

"I was looking for you for the same reason."

We walked along San Juan de Letrán Street. Just them a policeman came over to us. "You are under arrest!" he said. We saw a comrade walking up to us with some flyers. "Long live the Communist Party!" I shouted; this was the signal that we were being arrested. The comrade walked away. He followed us to see where we were being taken, and went to tell the Party that we were in jail.

At that time, Manuel, my husband, was thinking about coming back to me. A day earlier he had come to the barracks to see me. He had told me that he loved me and had never met another woman like me. He said that he was tired of people who only wanted him for his money. He said that he would come see me the next day so we could talk about things in more detail. I waited for him, but he never came. Since he wasn't living with me at the time, I couldn't have cared less. Imagine my surprise when I was taken to headquarters and found him there. "What are you doing here?" he asked me.

"Me—what about you?"

"Well, they arrested me when I was leaving the barracks, and that's why I never went back to see you, like I said I would. But why did they arrest you?"

"Same as usual, you know."

"Jesus, what luck."

The police came, pushing us along. "Get going, señora!"

"Wait just a minute, and don't touch me," I said to the police. "I'll go when I feel like it ... because that's how we Communists are."

"What do you mean, wait a minute? You're not in charge here!"

"Let the sun fall out of the sky, but I'm not moving!"

I finally went to my cell. When I was alone I thought how now I would lose my job with the cashier. But so what, I thought, my husband is coming back to me and at least he'll give me food and I won't have to work ... or at least until he leaves me again! Because I knew what a ladies' man he was and as soon as he found another one ... I'd be alone again!

He got out of jail first. He behaved very well. He went to see the other comrades so those of us who had been arrested would be let out. When I got out, we once again had a good life.

By then he had joined the Trotskyites. One day he brought Diego Rivera to our house on Dr. Lavista Street. He introduced him to me. I was afraid of that elephant at first; I didn't know him yet, and he was so ugly. "He's the painter I've talked about so much," Manuel explained.

"Pleased to meet you, señor. Please sit down."

I still didn't know much about politics. They started talking about Trotsky. I wonder who that is, I said to myself; and then the painter left. I was asleep when Manuel came to bed. "What an ugly man!" I said to him.

"Yes," he said, "but he's very intelligent."

"Oh, and the one who you were talking about ... Troy's horse, who's that?"

"You mean Trotsky? You don't know who he is? He's the one who won the war in Russia. But listen, I never said anything about any Troy's horse ... "

"Well, I don't know how to say his last name."

One day Manuel said: "It's time for you to go to your session. I want you to tell me later what it was about, because I want to be up on all the activities ... you know how things are."

I went to the session. I told him everything that had gone on. Another time he said to me, "I don't know what's going to happen, because now they're accusing me of being a Trotskyite."

"And what does that mean?" I asked him.

"It means I belong to the Party of the man I told you won the war in Russia."

"Well why should anything happen, if everyone's in the struggle for the same thing?"

"Don't be silly; don't you know he's fighting with Stalin?"

"I don't understand any of this."

He left. "They want to kick me out of the Party," he said when he returned home.

"So what did you say?"

"I tried to defend myself. When you go to your session, don't say anything about it if they ask you."

"About what, I don't understand anything."

"About that man ... "

"Tell us where the Trotskyites meet," a Party comrade said to me.

"But I don't even know what Trotskyites are."

"Of course you do; we know your husband is one."

"What? He's always with me and never stays away from home. Don't go accusing my husband of new vices. His only one is other women, but that's it."

"Look, we're going to explain to you who Trotsky is: he's a man who at one time was unintentionally on the side of the workers, but later he betrayed the revolution."

"Oh sure, I remember: he was at our house the other day. Of course! Yes, I know him. The next time he comes, I'll throw him out."

"But he isn't here in Mexico."

"Of course he is; I'll tell you what he looks like: a round face with bulging eyes ... "

"No, I tell you the man isn't in Mexico ... Another day when we have more time we'll tell you who Trotsky is and explain about Trotskyism. But right now we're talking about your man, who is a traitor. You, as a good Communist, should tell us what you know about him."

"I don't know anything. It's God's truth, I don't know a thing."

"Fine, but from now on pay attention to what he does and if he asks you anything about what went on here, don't tell him."

"I already know; he told me you want to kick him out, and after everything he's done for the struggle."

"Don't get angry, just watch him carefully."

"Don't count on it; he asked me to do the same with you."

"Oh he did? What did he say?"

"I won't tell you, because then you'll say that I'm a traitor."

"So at least now we know he's a declared Trotskyite," the comrades said, and then they said goodbye. "See you later!"

Back at home, my man started in on the same thing: "What happened, what went on?"

"Nothing! I'm no traitor, either to you or to them. I won't tell you anything. For me, I'll keep my affairs to myself."

"Look," he said,"if you want to keep your comfortable life you'll have to tell me everything that goes on in the Party. I'll leave you if you don't!"

"Don't come to me with your stories. You have another woman and that's why you want to leave!"

THE ASHES OF J.A. MELLA

At that time, the Party was organizing the shipment of Julio Antonio Mella's ashes to Cuba. The repression was at its height. Mella's ashes had been placed in a wooden box to be sent to Havana, but since we knew the police would try to get it away from us, the Party made two wooden boxes, exactly the same, to throw them off the track. In one of them we put the ashes and then hid it well in a safe place. The other box, the empty one, was used for the public events that were being planned. The Party organized a big meeting in the amphitheater of the high school, with the idea of paying one last homage to Julio Antonio's ashes before they left Mexico. The amphitheater was packed. The meeting began. Juan Marinello from Cuba spoke first, and Valentín S. Campa, from the Political Bureau of the Mexican Communist Party, and Manuel García Rodríguez, and others. Naturally the speeches were against the Portes Gil government, accomplice in Julio Antonio's assasination.

Before the ceremony was over, the police were at the door of the amphitheater, trying to get in so they could grab the urn that held Mella's ashes. Nobody knew that the ashes weren't in that box, except for the Party Political Bureau and the committee in charge of taking them to Cuba, a group which included Marinello, Rodolfo Dorantes, and another comrade. When the police arrived, Enrique Peña, thinking like everyone else that the ashes were in that urn, started running, grabbed the urn, and went to hide it. The police went after him and surrounded him. He passed the box to another comrade and the urn was passed from hand to hand, kept from the police, who were furious. "The box!" they were shouting. "Get the box! There it is!" But the box had disappeared.

I had brought some rotten eggs with me, just in case; I knew I might need them. And, in fact, as I was going down the stairs, I saw that people were already being grabbed by the police. Without hesitation, I smashed an egg in the face of the closest policeman. He ran over into a corner and began to vomit. I stayed in front, smashing eggs on the police, until they recognized me. "Get Benita!" they screamed. Then there were four police on top of me. They got me by the arms and legs after a terrible struggle. I got loose from them for a moment and started kicking all around. One of them fainted. When they tried to grab me again, I jumped on top of one of them, but he stabbed me in the arm with his bayonet. Finally they got me into a "Julia" wagon with the others who had been arrested. They were Juan Marinello, the lawyer Enrique González Aparicio, Germán Lizt Arzubide, Juan de la Cabada, Mirta Aguirre, the Proenza sisters, Catalina Peña, and many other comrades. There was also some Chinese man there; nobody knew him. They took our statements when we got to headquarters. The Chinese man was the first to report."

"What is your name?"

"Wang kom nan song pang ga mau," the Chinese man burst out in Chinese.

"Don't you speak Spanish?"

"Pote gim go kom pang san mom."

Nothing. The Chinese man was adamant. Then they sent for another Chinese so he could interpret. They asked him something in his language. The Chinese man started speaking in English. The men in headquarters realized he was trying to fool them, and they were furious. "Put him in a cell!"

"No! Why to cell? I protest!" he said in Spanish.

"I thought you couldn't speak Spanish, you miserable Chinese!"

"I no do anything! I pass by, coincidence . . . "

"We'll give you a coincidence!" the agents said.

"I honorable. Own cafe. Communists always in trouble; I passing by, they grab me . . . "

"Let me see your passport."

The passport was in order. "Fine, you're free to go." Then they started in on us. I hadn't realized that my arm was hurt. "What happened to you?" someone asked me. "Look at your arm!" Then I got mad all over again. I climbed up on a bench and started a meeting right there in police headquarters. I attacked the Portes Gil government repeatedly, until they finally locked me in my cell and I gave up.

But for Sotomayor, filling the "Julias" with Communists wasn't enough; he had to keep looking for the coffer that held Mella's ashes. He forced open the locks on the doors of the high school so he could search all the rooms. He ran all over the place, until he finally found a box in an empty water tank on the roof. He opened it and found a piece of paper inside. "Since we expected this sort of outrage," it said, "we put Mella's ashes in a safe place."

Today the ashes of Julio Antonio Mella rest on Cuban soil.

At that time, the City Pullman office was organizing a reception for a group of capitalists from Wall Street, Rotaries or something. The Party wrote some material criticizing these people, and commissioned me to hand it out. I went straight to the houses in Buenavista and placed the propaganda on the cars in the area where the millionaire tourists lived. The police quickly began to chase me. But I managed to escape and climbed over the fence at the the Buenavista police station. From that height I called a meeting. The police tried to get me down by pulling on my legs, but I kicked them and kept them away. The townspeople were on my side: "Let her go!" they shouted, "She can get down by herself!" They finally got me down and took me to jail.

I was there for three days. The day I got out the comrades arrived with more propaganda, this time against Hitler. It was to be pasted up that night. I prepared the *atole* mixture for pasting and got ready to go out on the street to post the flyers. There were two men staying in my house who were very broke. I was feeding them, but when I got out of jail I told them to look for somewhere else to go because I couldn't have them there anymore. Thinking that the police would give them something, they went to denounce me. They told the police that I had more propaganda and that I also had weapons in my house, and that many Communists met there. The day that I was going to go paste up the flyers, at about three o'clock in the afternoon, a swarm of police arrived to search my house. I was asleep. I didn't realize that the police were there until my daughter Lilia woke me up. "Open this closet!" they said.

"Just let me get my valuables first, because I know all about you thieves."

There was a great ruckus in the neighborhood when they saw so many police at my house. "What did you do, Benita?" the people asked me. "Kill someone?"

All they found was the propaganda. They led me to jail. My daughter started crying. She jumped on top of the policemen. "Don't take my mama away," she screamed. "Tomorrow is Three Kings Day and if you take her then there won't be anyone to buy me my presents. Besides, she was going to register me for school . . . now she won't be able to. Let her go!"

I signaled to my daughter to calm herself down and to stay

where she was, so she could tell the Party and the comrades to stay away from our house since my street was being watched. My daughter understood and was quiet. Some of my neighbors, seeing the girl left alone, wanted to take her home with them, but Lilia refused. "No," she said, "I have to stay home to attend to our guests, because if I don't then they'll leave and my mother will be very angry when she comes back." A few days later I was set free.

THE SHARPIE

But we didn't get out of jail in order to rest. In those days the Party had very few members and those few had to do everything. There were many tasks: call meetings, help the strikers, recruit factory workers, distribute propaganda, make paste-ups and paint on the walls at night and sell "El Machete," the Party newspaper. The central organ of the Party had not stopped publishing, despite the persecutions, despite vandalization of its press, despite the fact that many comrades had been put in jail for selling it or reading it. Who knows how they did it, but our "sharpie" was always in the hands of the workers, in the factories, and even in the barracks with the soldiers. At moments when it seemed like the Party was going to fall apart, the Calles government's every attack, jailing and sending the Communists to Islas Marias, "El Machete" would appear, encouraging people, giving the necessary directives for work, giving everyone enough confidence and faith to continue in the struggle, knowing that there was a Central Committee that would not lose heart, that even while hidden away would work and keep alive the flame of enthusiasm.

I didn't read the "sharpie" because it was very difficult for me, since I could barely join letters together, but Manuel would read it to me at night and explain the things I didn't understand. I liked him to read it to me because his explanations made things very clear. I felt a great love for the sharpie. That's why I felt proud and happy the first time they commissioned me to go out and sell it. I felt that the Central Committee had confidence in me and had given me a very important task.

The sharpie was distributed in Mexico City by a Polish comrade who had joined the Party in Mexico. We called him Bota-Botas; I don't know why, but everyone knew him by this name; nobody knew his real one. One time, comrade Bota-Botas landed in jail for selling the sharpie, along with some other comrades. When a foreigner is arrested, they have the right to deport him. The police called him for his statement. "Name?"

"Carlos Rosas," Bota-Botas said, just to say something, but he said it with a foreign accent that gave it all away.

"Are you a Mexican?"

"Sí, señor!"

"Where are you from?"

"I am from the stake of Michoacán."

The police roared with laughter. "What did you say?" they asked him again.

"The *stake*?"

"Yes; the stake of Michoacán."

For some reason he was not deported and he continued to distribute the sharpie.

When they gave me my first bundle of papers to sell, I felt great. I got up early the next morning to fix Manuel's breakfast and had everything ready by nine o'clock. Manuel ate his breakfast, I cleaned up around the house, and then went out to sell the paper.

I went to San Juan de Letrán Street. I was so proud to be carrying "El Machete," I started yelling out loud. I wanted everyone to know I had the sharpie. When I sold my first copy I really felt something special. But I soon noticed some police coming up behind me. I started to run. The police came running after me. They'll kill me first, I thought, but they're not going to get the paper away from me. I stuck the ones I had left down my shirt. The agents were chasing me around the stands on San Juan, but since there were so many people they couldn't reach me.

I kept selling and before noon I had sold them all and could go home in time to give Manuel his lunch. When they saw I had sold all the papers, they gave me more and commissioned me to sell in the factories in La Carolina and El Anfora. It was more difficult there. At the time, some labor leaders were making a great effort against the Communists and had managed to mislead the workers. Sometimes, when we would go to the factories to sell the paper, the workers would insult us. "El Machete, comrades, the worker's newspaper!"

"Hey mama, you're cute!" they would say to me. "I'll buy your paper if you go out with me tonight, what d'ya say?"

But there were others who bought from us. Another time, when were were having a meeting in front of La Carolina to sell the sharpie, some workers, stirred up by the reformist leaders, threw water at us; we were soaked completely. We didn't pay any attention to them and kept on talking. Then some other workers took our side. "Stop the bullshit!" they said. "That's no way to treat women . . . " The others answered them back and the riot began. They started fighting and many people were hurt.

We also sold the sharpie at demonstrations. There were men among the crowd who would curse at us. Many times we ran away near tears, seeing that our brothers, own brothers, were treating us this way, but when we met up with workers who respected us and who knew how to treat us like comrades, we would forget everything else. What did it matter? We had to make sacrifices so our dear sharpie would get into the hands of the workers, and so that the Communist Party could maintain contact with the masses. They had given us this task and we carried it out with pride . . .

CONSUELO'S GREEN EYES

It was the anniversary of the Russian Revolution. It was a date commemorated more than any other. The Party organized a meeting in the Pirata Salon, on San Miguel Street. When I arrived, the event had already begun. Since I had just gotten out of prison and I didn't want them to get me again, I had found myself a very elegant hat that I could hide under. The first person I noticed when I got to the meeting was Sotomayor, disguised as a paper-seller, with a patch over one eye. There were many other disguised police present. It starting going around the room that there were some police there and someone told the speakers.

Ten minutes later they started arresting people. The battle was on. When the meeting was over, the agents posted themselves at the door to see the people who were leaving and to detain the Communists. I disguised myself, putting on the hat. I looked quite the bourgeois and I went out, thinking the agents wouldn't recognize me. Then I passed in front of them.

"Benita," they said, "take off the hat; we already know who you are."

"Well you creeps, I know who you are, too; did you really think you were disguised?"

We went back to police headquarters. The same as always; questions and more questions. "What is your name?" and, "What is she here for?"

Fingerprints and everything. They got a whole group of us: Consuelo Uranga, Rosa Pérez, Pedro Juliac and many others. Of course the charge was insulting the Head Magistrate!

At the same time, the police had arrested a *gringo* who was tricking people with a machine for finding treasure. They put the *gringo* in a cell near ours. They took Consuelo and some other women at midnight to see Chief Belén. The next day, the *gringo* started shouting.

"Consuelo! Consuelito!" . . . I'm going to say I'm Consuelo, I thought to myself, and have a little fun with this *gringo*.

"Here I am!" I answered him. "But who told you my name was Consuelo?"

"Oh! I know it when they take your statement," he said in broken Spanish.

"And why are you here, you poor bandit?"

"Oh no! I am not bandit. I business man. And you, why you here?"

"For being a Communist!"

"Oh, very bad!"

We stopped talking and then the *gringo* started to shout again. "Hey, Consuelo! Do you have a mattress?"

"No!"

"And soap?"

"No soap either!"

"Have you eaten?"

"Well what do you know, I haven't eaten yet!"

The *gringo* had a lot of money, and made them bring me a new mattress, some Palmolive soap, and sent for a meal from the Regis restaurant, with jello, chicken, and a ton of other good things. My comrades and I were happy as clams. I shared the food the *gringo* had sent me with the other comrades. We were living the good life!

"Consuelito!" the *gringo* shouted again.

"What's up?"

"Did you get the things I sent you?"

"Yes, much appreciated."

"You know what, Consuelito? I much in love with you."

"Well, that's great! I'm in love with you, too."

"Yes? When you in love with me?"

"When they were taking your fingerprints."

"Oh, no an opportune moment."

The *gringo* was very stupid and didn't realize I was having fun with him. For a time, he kept falling more in love, sending me breakfast, lunch, and Regis dinners on a tray, magnificent meals. And eight days went by.

"Consuelito!"

"What is it?"

"I'm going to ask move to other cell, closer to yours."

"But why? Aren't you comfortable there?"

"Yes, but want to see again your green eyes . . . "

Well that was that, I thought. So much for the dinners from Regis! We would go back to the mess the jail gave us. Since the *gringo* had money, he managed to get moved to a cell in front of ours. A few days later he introduced himself to us. I laid down, with my face toward the wall so he wouldn't see me. "Consuelito!"

"What do you want?"

"I want see you."

"I'm sick. Don't bother me."

But I couldn't avoid having the *gringo* see me. "Oh, you no Consuelo!"

"Yeah, so what!"

"You very ugly . . . bad person! Cheating me for one week . . . bandit!"

He was furious. He send me to hell in English and in Spanish. He asked them to move him back to the cell he was in before. But for eight days, the name and the green eyes of Consuelo Uranga brought us food as we had never enjoyed before!

Some say what I did was wrong, others say it was good to use the *gringo*. The only thing I know is that the other prisoners were very happy when the trays came from the Regis. And later I thought: Anyway, the *gringo* got his money by stealing from Mexicans, so it's only fair that Mexicans enjoy it . . .

ERRORS OF THE PARTY

Manuel had come back to me so he could use me as a spy, but I fooled him, because when I found out what Trotskyism was I was put on my guard and I started to watch his movements. There was a Spanish man named Manuel Grandioso. "Look, comrade," he said to me, "you should be on our side, because the Communists want to kill the man who made the revolution and you could be very useful to us." So that was the fight between my husband and the Party. I didn't say anything to anyone about anything. One of them told me he was right. The others said that they were. Finally one day the Party said that if I didn't leave Manuel they would throw me out. What could I do?

In those days, Manuel had gotten interested in sports. He joined the YMCA. He went swimming every day. He never wanted to leave the gym because he was seeing a woman there. So, I decided to leave him peacefully. We separated. He went with the other woman, but this time he left me money and furniture. One day the Party called a session. When I arrived they had already started. They were arguing and talking about throwing out all the Trotskyites. I was against it. I proposed that they give them hard work to test them out. Then Revueltas, the secretary of the group, said to me, "Look, Benita, if you're against it, we'll kick you out, too."

"Brother, you're no one. The Central Committee is the only . . . "

"But as their representative, I declare that all Trotskyites are expelled and you are also expelled."

"Look, you bastard, you're not going to throw me out."

"Oh yes I am!"

"Here's your yes I am . . . "

I jumped on top of him and we went at each other with all our might.

I didn't pay attention to Revueltas' throwing me out. I continued in the struggle as always. I went to jail for taking part in the bus drivers' strike in Tacuba. I wanted to show them with deeds that I would continued to be a revolutionary above all else. As for the expulsion, I considered it Revueltas' problem and nothing more. I did feel that the Party committed errors, but that it was wise enough to correct them and continue in the struggle against the bourgeoisie.

As for me, I had managed to pull myself away from the cabaret and to awaken my revolutionary conscience; I had made myself understand just what my role was in capitalist society: it was on the side of the workers. And it wasn't because the Party bothered itself much to educate its members. On the contrary, I criticize how it ignores the men and women who fight for it. They don't take much time to educate people. I use myself as an example of that.

I saw that the most capable and intelligent comrades were those who treated their comrades the worst, scornfully, and without taking the time to educate them, betraying the female comrades with other women, just like any petit-bourgeois, yet they were the first to say, "She's a whore!" when the woman found another man.

I, who had wanted to be an example for the comrades, have not achieved that goal because I have had so many disadvantages; for example, the disgrace of not being able to read; this is one of my biggest disabilities. But I don't blame the Party for this . . . Well, in part I do, because when the Party was strong, they could have taken the time to educate me politically, but they didn't. Other times I went to ask them to help me find a job. I asked different comrades, and even though the situation of the Party was good in those days, they didn't pay any attention to me. I felt sad when I realized that people who hadn't even struggled for our Party had good jobs . . . this didn't discourage me because I understood that I couldn't give the Party the amount of work that other more capable comrades could. "Why don't you go see comrade Laborde?" someone would say to me.

"No, not that."

Laborde is our chief, I thought to myself. His work is to orient the struggle of our Party, not to bother himself with the small things that happen to us. How important could Benita Galeana be to him, and whether or not she had a job?

It's true that at times, when my own situation got very bad, I would say to myself: "I have now been working with the Communist Party for many years. I've gone to jail fifty-eight times for the struggle. I've suffered hunger, privations, persecutions. I have almost gone blind and I've risked my life many times for the Party.

But to this day, they haven't bothered themselves for me. In all the years I've been fighting, I haven't had one word, not one bit of friendliness from the chief of my Party. And there's more; although it's unbelievable, in all these years of the struggle, I have not had so much as a "Good morning, Benita," from Laborde.

I know I'm no one in the Party. A member of the line, politically backward. But I never felt that the leaders of the Party showed any interest in helping to direct me, in bettering my revolutionary work, in making me, by guiding and stimulating me to make me a more conscientious and capable worker. I have felt that they left me alone in my ignorance.

In my years of active struggle with the Party I did make some friends, because I have lived all my life in contact with people. Sometimes, when they would introduce me at a meeting, the people would shout, "We want the comrade with the braids to speak!" I was the comrade with the braids, because that's how I wore my hair, like village women, and the people trusted me for that, and also surely for my way of speaking, a way they could understand very easily. The Party could have used these things, making me a more capable and better-oriented revolutionary . . . but they never paid attention to me.

Later, when I was about to quit the Party for my great love for Humberto, no one said, "We can't lose Benita!" Instead they just started saying, "Benita's been lost, she's become a bourgeois!" They didn't help me to develop, and I believe that this is how they have treated all the comrades.

But in spite of these things, I continued with the same faith in my Party, knowing that it was capable of correcting its errors, because it allows criticism. Later I thought: if the Party, with all its errors, has managed to transform my life, pulling me out of vice and sin, just think what it could do if only it corrected these errors!

LIFE WITH THE COMRADES

I was then living with Manuel's mother. One night I bumped into Juan de la Cabada. "I want to take you out to the movies," he said.

"But I can't get home late."

"Fine, we'll go out early."

We went to the Iris Theater. As we were leaving we saw Pedro Juliac. "Where are you going?" he asked us.

"I'm taking Benita home," Cabada said, "because she has to be in early."

"But I've got some money, and I want to take you both out for some *tortas*."

"Are you sure they aren't 'running *tortas*?'"

In those underground days, the young men of the Party lived in terrible poverty. They didn't have enough to eat. Those were some hungry times! So, a group of student Communists, Pedro Juliac, Rodolfo Dorantes, Enrique Ramírez y Ramírez, José Revueltas, Carlos Rojas Juanco, Raúl Calvo, Ignacio León and others, had started going to cafes and restaurants and ordering something to eat. When they had filled themselves, they would take off running. They called these "running coffees" or "running suppers," depending on what it was. One time, when the Spanish writers Rafael Alberti and María Teresa León came to Mexico, the young Communists offered to take them to a "running banquet," with the only difference being that, since they were the guests of honor, the students would give them a half-hour advantage to run off before the trouble started. Later, the Political Bureau of the Party began criticizing the young men for these kinds of things and the "running coffees" stopped. But in those days, they were still taking place.

"No, seriously," Juliac said, "I've got some money."

"Good, let's go."

We were at a street stand, and by the time we realized it, it had gotten late. "Now what can I do?" I said, "I can't go home now. Besides, I'm too embarrassed to wake up the señora." The boys didn't have anywhere to sleep, either. "Well," said Juliac, "I know a hotel on Colombia; they have rooms for seventy-five *centavos*. We could take one if you want." We went and asked for a room.

The hotel keeper was staring at us. "What? One woman for two men?" he said.

"Of course!" Juliac said. "This woman is worth two . . . even three."

The man couldn't understand that a woman could sleep with two men . . . as comrades. I lay down in the corner, then Cabada lay down, and then Juliac. The next day, as we were leaving, the hotel keeper was still intrigued, looking me up and down. "Who knows what that old creep is imagining," I said to them.

"What else can he imagine—that we had a *menage a trois*," Juliac said.

We went out onto the street, and each one went his way.

Seeing what a bad situation I was in, without work, with no money, and alone, I thought to myself: So, will I have to go back to my old life now? No! I'll look for a job, even if it's as a caretaker . . . but since I was well known as a Communist, no one wanted to give me work. The struggle against Calles continued, and against the National Revolutionary Party. I kept fighting alongside my comrades. Nobody took my expulsion seriously or spoke about it again. Whenever there was a meeting, I was the first one to be thrown in jail, because all the police knew me well, since I always fought with them.

After being tossed in jail a few times, I went out onto the street. I found myself without money, without knowing what to do. Hungry. This was no life. Then I decided to go back to the cabaret, with a shame that made me want to die. I felt disgust seeing how they exploited the workers there who went to spend their pay, and I was ashamed to see my female comrades and how they were exploited by the owner of the cabaret, who charged them five *pesos* every time they went out with a friend. I felt even more anger against the capitalist regime that was responsible for all these things. I will keep fighting with the Communist Party, I said to myself, even harder than before, until the bourgeois regime is over.

One day an agent from the reserves introduces himself to me. "Hey!" he said, "What are you doing here? Aren't you a Communist anymore?"

"What do you care?" I answered.

Jesus! It's truly a shame that we revolutionaries have so few ways to earn a living. And then the bourgeoisie uses that to attack us. One night a *gringo* came to the cabaret and invited me to have a drink. I knew I shouldn't drink, so I said no. He insisted, but I wouldn't drink. So he sat down to talk instead. He left at two in the morning. "Since you didn't want to drink anything," he said when he left, "I want to leave you some money. I'll see you tomorrow." The next day he went to my house to invite me to take a walk. I accepted. We went out walking. Then he asked me if I wanted to be his woman. "I'll think about it!" I answered.

"But do it quickly, because I'm leaving. I'm the manager of El Aguila and I live in Tampico. I have to leave soon."

I thought that if I went with him I would have to quit the movement, but I preferred to leave town rather than continue at the cabaret. I accepted and we went to live in Tampico. He set up a beautiful house for me with a lot of furniture. There were two Chinese servants, and one just for me, just to take care of me. The *gringo* loved me very much, to exaggeration. I didn't have to do anything and I had everything I wanted . . . even luxuries! But one day I received a letter from Manuel, saying he was in prison and would I go get him out. I tore up the letter and didn't answer it. A few days later I got another letter. "Benita," it said, "I think about you more than ever, because it is in jail and in bed where one really knows who his friends are. But I know that he who lives by the sword dies by the sword. I only want to be your advisor, your guardian angel. I know you're doing very well; all I ask is that you come get me out. I know you'll do it, because I know you well; I know you'll find a way . . . "

When the *gringo* came home I told him everything and asked him for money so I could go to Mexico City to get Manuel out of jail. Since the *gringo* love me so much, and never denied me anything, he gave it to me, but on the condition that I return to him. I promised and then I came to Mexico City. I went to see Manuel. He named me as his defending counsel so I could go into the prison anytime I wanted. He told me what I had to do: to go see the judge and some other things. Finally he got out. Then he wanted us to get back together. I told him that my getting him out of jail didn't mean anything, and that I wouldn't go back to him; in the first place because, being a Trotskyite he didn't deserve a revolutionary woman to bother with him. "So what are you going to do?" he asked me. "Are you going to go back to Tampico?"

"No, because what I want more than anything is my liberty; I don't want to depend on anybody. I will continue fighting just as

I always have, beneath the flag of the Communist Party."

"I'll help you," Manuel said.

But we separated, and this was the last time. I couldn't go back to Manuel, who had become a shameless Trotskyite. I couldn't forgive him for having betrayed the cause of the workers. I lost all respect for him after that.

And speaking of people who have betrayed the cause, I remember Rubén Salazar Mallén very clearly. In those days, Salazar Mallén had joined the Party. At the time, the meetings were held in the homes of sympathizers or comrades. On a few occasions we had sessions at Salazar Mallén's house, which was near Venezuela Street. We almost always ended up fighting with him at these sessions, because the more things were explained to him, the less he understood about Party tactics and other matters. They say it was his love for a comrade that had brought him to the Party. It must have been so, because he never agreed with the Party line. Sometimes we would talk about it. "I believe you think the way you do because you're ill. People with physical defects can become very envious. If you weren't crippled . . . "

"I . . . I would still feel the same," he answered in a thick voice.

The comrade he was in love with got him interested in the struggle, thinking it would surely be good for the Party to have an intellectual like Salazar Mallén among them. When she walked with him, she took him by the arm, on the side where he limped, making her limp, too. At the sessions, when she had to stand up for something, she would limp for Salazar Mallén. Finally, and since he never to understood the Party line and also because his relationship did not continue with the comrade he was courting, they made a plan to throw him out of the Party. Sometimes I would see him on the street.

"Benita," he would say, "I see you're out of jail . . . "

"Yes," I answered, "but I haven't seen you anywhere at all."

"It's because I admire you from afar. You're brave. You're always ready to fight."

Even after his expulsion he would come to our meetings, until one time the workers threw him out of the high school amphitheater. His betrayal of the revolution and his friendship with the Brown Shirts had made everyone hate him.

"How are you, Benita?" he said the last time I saw him. "Are you still brave? Are you still working in the struggle under your comrades?"

   "Not under," I said to him, "alongside them!"

   He invited me to the Paris Café. I declined the invitation.

THE HUNGER STRIKE

I continued in the struggle of the Communist Party with growing enthusiasm. The repression continued. We constantly fought with the police. One one occasion they appointed Revueltas and me to call some meetings demanding the liberty of other comrades who were in prison in Santiago. Revueltas and I were working on this, over by the Arcos de Belén, when they arrested us and took us to headquarters. They had us there for a while and then they drove us in a private car to the National Palace, where the other arrested comrades were. When we arrived, they had already taken everyone's testimony; we were the only ones left. They took me it first to testify. The man who took the statement was a military man who didn't know us. "Señorita," he asked me, "why have they arrested you?"

"Oh, señor!" I said. "I have no idea. I was speaking to this young man who is a friend of my family. I was asking about his brothers and sisters when the police arrived and arrested him; 'But what did you do?' I asked him, 'Did you rob someone?' And then the police man, without another word, said 'Let's go' to both of us."

I played my role well and the military man shook his head.

"How rude!" he said. These police agents commit every kind of abuse; it's frightening. You are a Catholic of course?"

The military man was looking at a little locket I wore around my neck, a memento from my family, and thought it was a saint or something from the church. At that moment I didn't know what to say. I didn't know if I should say I was a Catholic or not. Revueltas made a sign with his eyes for me to say yes.

"Yes, very Catholic." I said.

"I can see that, by your locket. No, I've always said that these police agents from headquarters only commit brutalities . . . this young woman is free as of this moment!" he ordered.

Just then a headquarters employee arrived, saying to the officer, "Here are the records of the detained Communists." Mine was right on top. I left the National Palace as fast as I could, hoping to run out into the street. When I reached the door, I felt someone coming up behind me. I ran faster. Then I felt someone grab me by the arm. "One moment, señorita," he said. They took me inside again. The military man stared at me angrily. "So you're very Catholic, eh?" he said. "What you are is a phony."

They took the other comrades away and left Revueltas and me. They didn't want to take everyone at once because they knew there would be a scene. Finally they gave the order to go. There was a thirty-man escort formed for us, soldiers with their bayonets raised, and an officer. They put Revueltas and me in the middle and gave the order to leave. Before we went, the officer said to me, "Señorita, I warn you to keep quiet, because if you provoke a scene I will find it necessary to use one of my weapons."

"Is that right?" I answered him. "Well if I had a weapon, both of us would be using them!"

Then the officer gave the order: "Arms up! Forward! March!" Out we went. There were some soldiers at the door of the National Palace. I can't waste this opportunity, I said to myself, and I began to shout: "Down with the government of Ortiz Rubio, who jails workers and sends them to Islas Marías! Long live the Communist Party of Mexico!"

I continued walking and shouting. There were many people gathered around. The officer didn't know what to do. He gave the order to halt and turn around. They took us back inside. They put us in a room and kept us there for a while. Then the officer came over to me. "Now, señorita," he said, "if you cause another scene, I promise you I will use my weapon."

"Fine," I said, "I promise I won't shout if you tell me where we're being taken."

"Agreed," he said. "We are taking you to Santiago."

I took advantage of the time they left us alone to grab a piece of cardboard, where I wrote as best I could: I have been arrested for being a Communist. I won't shout, I said to myself, but this sign is going right on my chest. Soon the soldiers lined up again and off we went . . .

I walked out the door of the National Palace quietly, as I had promised, but once we were on Moneda Street and I saw so many people I just couldn't hold it in and I started shouting for death to the Ortiz Rubio government, death to the bourgeoisie, and I put my sign on my chest. The people around us started shouting, too. "Let them go!" they were saying.

"Let them go!" I was wearing a long brown charmeusse silk dress, very beautiful and elegant. "I've never seen a woman dressed like that being taken away by so many soldiers!" the people were saying.

Then people started following us. There were more and more of them. The soldiers were afraid that the crowd would attack them, to make them free us. They were opening the way by hitting people with the butts of their rifles, because the crowd would barely let us go forward. I was still shouting against the government that killed peasants and jailed workers, and all the other Party slogans.

The people were shouting, too, louder and louder: "Let them go! What could these young people have done!" "She looks just like Mata Hari!" some women up on the sidewalk were saying, "Just like when they were taking her away to be executed!"

An old woman, making her way through the crowd and the lines of soldiers, came up to me and hugged me. "You didn't do anything wrong, did you, my dear?" she said, crying, her wrinkled face full of tears.

It gave me a lump in my throat.

When we reached Santiago prison, there were about two hundred people accompanying us. When we got close to the army barracks the people started going after the soldiers so they would let us go. The official had to ask for help from the garrison at Santiago. Then we finally arrived.

Revueltas went with the male comrades and I went with the women.

"Here comes Benita for a visit," they said when they saw me. "What did you bring us?"

"What can I bring you, when I'm here as a prisoner!"

We talked for a while and agreed to have a meeting to decide what to do. It was said that they were going to send all of us to Islas Marías in a few days.

At the meeting we agreed to declare a hunger strike in protest. One day we saw the lawyer Carlos Zapata Vela and Pedro Juliac coming; they were there for some court matters. I thought they were there to visit us.

"Girls," I said to my comrades, "quick, here comes the boys to visit us." Everyone ran out. The men walked past us. "Did you know we're going on a hunger strike?" I said to them. Zapata Vela answered me in a very serious tone.

"I don't know anything," he said, "and besides, I don't know who you are, señorita."

Juliac didn't say anything. Both of them, who are very dark, had turned completely white in the face. Juliac was pretending to be a notary, someone named Zapata Vela. "Shut up!" one of the comrades said. "Now you've ruined everything!"

They went into the office and came out soon after. Their faces were dark again. On the way out they said, "Goodbye girls, and good luck."

We decided to work on the soldiers. We told them we were going on a hunger strike and asked them to go to the newspapers and tell them. That afternoon the press had the news: Fifty Communists on Hunger Strike. That was the sign we were waiting for so we could begin our strike. The next day when they brought us our breakfast, we threw the trays and the plates on the ground. "We don't want anything to eat. We're calling a hunger strike!" we said. Then we called a meeting, singing "The International", and calling down with Ortiz Rubio and long live the Communist Party of Mexico. We attacked the officers and defended the soldiers, who at that time only earned one *peso* and forty *centavos*. We talked to the soldiers about their families' poverty, about their shoeless children who couldn't go to school . . .

The soldiers came to us in solidarity, but the officers gave the order for us to be locked up again. Our souls were burning. We grabbed the door of our cell and began shaking it with all our might. When they heard the noise, the prison director showed up, along with various officials and soldiers. One of the officials took out his sword and ordered the soldiers to separate us and send us to "Cartuchos." "We won't leave here," we said, "and if we go, we're going together."

"I'll make damn sure you leave!" the official said.

He ordered the soldiers to get us out. We grabbed cans, chamber pots, plates, everything we had on hand, and we stood in front of the officials. "And we'll make damn sure you won't make us leave, and if you do, you'll have to take us out dead!" we said to him.

One of the comrades had the idea for us to ask to speak to Evelio Vadillo. The prison director accepted, to put an end to the scene. Evelio arrived. "What's going on, girls?"

"They want to separate us," we answered.

"Don't let them, comrades. All women Communists must stay together and die together, if necessary."

Then, directing the soldiers, he called a meeting. He talked to them about their economic problems and how they should join the workers' struggle. Then, to finish it off, he walked over to the officials. "Let the Communists stay together," he said. "I will make sure there are no more problems!"

During the hunger strike the soldiers were on our side. They listened to us carefully when we talked to them, and they applauded. Sometimes they would shout, "Long live the Communists!" Then, when the soldiers who were imprisoned in rooms facing the courtyard started to take our side, they locked them up again in their cells. But they would shout from inside. "Hurray for the hunger strike!" they would say.

And even the free soldiers who were around would greet us with happy faces. We were enchanted by them, because they treated us so well. We would shout to them, too. "Hurray for the soldiers who are on the side of the workers and who will soon help us to take over!"

"Hurray for the female Communists!" they would answer.

Then the chiefs and the officials would come out to calm the soldiers. But they managed to keep in contact with us. They offered to go buy things we needed. They were very good to us. When we were suspicious of one of them we would ask: "You aren't going to denounce us?"

"I'm no rat!"

"Soldier's word?"

"Soldier's word!"

"Communist's word?"

"Communist's word!"

Not one of them ever betrayed us.

We continued our hunger strike for one week, Margarita Gutiérrez, María Luisa de Carrillo, a Jewish woman named Dina, Catalina Peña, and I. Once the sound of a cornet woke us up at five in the morning. "Girls, girls!" the soldiers were shouting. "They're taking the Communists to Manzanillo!" They had taken them out at midnight so we wouldn't find out. They were taking them all to Islas Marías: Gómez Lorenzo, José Revueltas, and others . . . and that same day they set us free.

The Jewish woman was deported. Margarita, Catalina and María Luisa left on foot. They had to carry me out because I was very weak. I felt sick. I went to see a friend who was a doctor. He gave me an injection and some grape juice. He kept me with him for three days. Then suddenly my sight went bad and I almost lost it. I couldn't move my eyes. They just stopped moving and then I couldn't walk. The ground seemed to be full of holes. Chan Urueta helped me buy some medicine. He also bought me my first eye glasses . . .

TWO FRIENDS

With the money I had left over from what the *gringo* from Tampico had given me, I rented a house at 31 Galeana Street, and I rented rooms and that helped me out some. One day an old man came to rent a room. His name was Luis Camargo and he was from a very rich family. He paid me fifty *pesos* a month for room and board. He was a very good person. He loved me and he used to take me out; he bought dresses for me and my daughter. He worked at the Supreme Court. He was about eighty years old.

When we went out for walks he would introduce me as his daughter. I loved him and took care of him when he got sick. He was grateful and told me he was going to leave me everything he had. He told me that when he was young he had fallen in love with a young girl. He had wanted to marry her, but his family was against it, because "she didn't belong to his class." Don Luis submitted to his family's wishes and he did not marry his girlfriend, but he swore that he would never love another woman and would never get married. The old man had kept to his word. He had never married, but instead he became a drunk. He drank all the time; he would have a glass of alcohol with cinammon at breakfast. But he never lost control and he was always very well-behaved.

Sometimes he would come home with streaks of rouge on his face, or else smelling of perfume. "What happened to you, don Guicho?" I would ask him.

"These women at the Court are driving me crazy; they've covered me with kisses. They want me to marry them."

"All of them?"

"Yes, all of them, and there are about a hundred . . . "

Don Guicho used to buy cakes of rouge, perfumes or lotions, and would dab his own face or put perfume on himself to make people think that the employees had kissed and hugged him. Other times he would talk to himself in his room, kiss his own hand loudly, or make his bedsprings squeak, hoping that I would hear him. The next day I would ask him: "Now, Guicho. What kind of mischief were you into last night, with so much noise and all that kissing?"

"So you heard something?"

"Of course I did; I was awake the whole time!"

"Well, a woman came over to see me!"

He liked to take me out to eat in elegant restaurants. "You behave yourself, you hear?" he would say before we went in. Sometimes we went to the Concordia. He would pick up the menu and order those dishes that are so hard to pronounce. "Señorita," I would say to the waitress, "some *tortillas*, please." Everyone at every table turned around to stare at me.

"But señora," the waitress would answer, "this food doesn't come with *tortillas*. We don't have *tortillas* here,"

Don Luis broke out in a cold sweat. He took out his handkerchief and wiped his forehead. I kept it up, teasing him and trying to make him angry. When the waitress came with the silverware, I would say out loud, so the other tables could hear: "And these pieces of steel? What are they for? Please bring me my food." The old man ate everything; he was very angry when we left. "Don't touch me!" he said.

"But why not, don Guicho?"

"Because you embarrassed me. I couldn't even touch my food . . . "

I was working in those days in a jewelry store, earning twenty-five *pesos* a month. One day a man came to have a bracelet made. He started staring at me. "Goddamn!" he said. "I've been looking for just this type of woman and look where I find her!" We started talking. He asked me where I was from, who my parents were, and things like that. He asked me to show him a tie clip with a gemstone that he liked, and then he said to the owner of the store, "I want to buy this, but on one condition."

"What is it?"

"That you send it to the house along with the young woman."

"Of course, my pleasure."

I went to deliver the tie clip. I thought the old man might have bad intentions. I arrived at his house. I knew who he was; his name was Francisco Iturbide and he was a millionaire. He was very attentive to me. He showed me his whole house. His collection of paintings, woodcuts, embossings, ones where he was the only model and appeared in different poses and situations; in some, going into church, in others, dressed like an Indian, in others, with a crown, at the moment of being crowned, or with an umbrella; it was a complete gallery of himself.

Next to this gallery he showed me a room where a woman named Anita had lived. He had a collection of paintings that showed Anita in all the stages of death: in bed, sick, gravely ill, dying, dead, laid out, in her coffin, on the road to the cemetery, and being lowered into the tomb. "How long ago did she die?" I asked him.

"She isn't dead; she just left; but for me it's as if she died."

He asked me whether I liked his paintings. "Not a single one," I said.

"Of course! They're for people who understand them."

When I left he gave me ten *pesos* as a tip for the delivery, and invited me to dinner at Sanborn's that same evening. "Come here," he said to me when I arrived. "I want to show you something." He took me over to the staircase, and stopped me in front of a mural by José Clemente Orozco. "Do you like this one?" he asked me.

"Yes, it's beautiful."

"But why do you like it?"

"I can't really say why; I just like it."

We went to eat; we talked and became friends. He gave me presents, and money, and dresses; he never asked for anything in return. He liked to take me to eat at the stands in the Lagunilla Market. Other times he would take the paperboys to dinner at the cafés on San Juan de Letrán and give them money. The boys loved him very much.

One time the actress Lola del Río came to Mexico City. Don Francisco called me on the telephone to invite me to dinner. "But wear your shawl and put your hair in braids," he said. He took me to Prendes. We sat down. He ordered the dinner. While they were bringing it, I saw a big group of people coming in. "Are there always this many people here?" I asked him.

"No. They're here because they want to see Lola del Río."

"Is she here?"

"Yes, she's the one dressed in black."

"But she's not talking to anyone."

"Of course she isn't. They're only here to look at her and admire her clothes and jewelry."

She was talking, and talking . . . in English, without paying any attention to the people. "Doesn't she know how to speak Spanish?" I asked don Francisco.

"Yes, but it looks like she's forgotten."

Don Francisco and I are still friends . . . but he's interested in me only as another picture missing from his collection.

THE DEATH OF BENJAMIN JIMÉNEZ

The struggle against Calles and Ortiz Rubio continued at full speed. The police barely gave us room to breathe. But the Party wasn't afraid of them. It called its meetings in spite of the police and any other opposition. One time they organized a meeting at the Mina movie theater. Hernán Laborde, the chief of our Party, was going to speak. They had taken precautions, because they thought the police might come to break it up.

The cops were after Laborde, so they sent undercover agents, and the Mexican President's special agents had orders to arrest him. When the meeting started, there were already many disguised agents in the room. Despite this, Laborde spoke out and the agents had to sit there and listen to the voice of the Communist Party, talking about all the movement's issues. They didn't dare arrest him inside the room and they waited until he went outside so they could get him on the street. We spread the word: "Keep your eyes on Laborde! Don't let Laborde get arrested!"

The meeting finished with great enthusiasm and cries of long live the Mexican Communist Party. I didn't see when Laborde disappeared because I was watching some disguised agents in the room; Laborde left without being arrested, but the agents on the street recognized him and followed him in a car. Benjamín Jiménez, who was in charge of the guard, went after the agents when he saw what was happening. He had an ax in his hands, one he had used to make signs.

The agents went after Laborde and tried to grab him when they got to Guatemala Street. Benjamín Jiménez arrived at that precise moment, and when an agent stopped Laborde, Jiménez swung the ax at him and knocked him down. Almost at the same time, one of the President's agents who was standing behind Laborde shot at Benjamín, who fell down, too; he was badly hurt. Laborde escaped and the police were left standing there.

Benjamín was taken to a Red Cross clinic. They tried to save him, they operated on him, but you could see that he wasn't going to survive. Then someone at the hospital took a priest to see him so he could confess. Jiménez refused. He didn't even want the priest to be there. When the priest came up to his bed, he sent him away.

Benjamín was very angry. The nurse brought him a glass of

water. Benjamín got worse and then he died. It was felt that the nurse gave him the water in bad faith, knowing it would be bad for him after the fit he had with the priest.

They took him from the Red Cross to the Alcázar funeral parlor, and he lay in state there for five days. They had to inject the cadaver to preserve it for several days. The Party wanted to make it an important burial. The police kept watching us, because they wanted to have the body buried quietly.

In another room at the same funeral parlor, they were holding a wake for a Japanese man. When they took him out, the police thought it was Benjamín Jiménez and went running after the Japanese man.

When we realized that the police wouldn't let us call a meeting in the cemetery, before beginning the funeral procession, we held a meeting in the room at the Alcázar, where Benjamín Jiménez's son, Mauro, spoke. At the time he was thirteen years old. He condemned his father's killers and swore that he would continue fighting for the Communist Party and against the capitalist regime.

The burial was organized, and four hundred of us walked along, singing Lenin's Funeral March, *The International*, and other revolutionary songs we knew. The police headed us off at El Caballito. We prepared to fight them; we knew they wanted to get Jiménez's body away from us. They used tear gas and broke our line. We fought back, but finally the police got possession of the body and quickly took it to the Dolores Cemetery. We followed them.

When we arrived, the police were surrounding the plot where Jiménez was going to be buried. They were lying on the ground, with rifles raised and aimed down at the tomb, ready to start a massacre if someone tried to call a meeting. The body was buried without any speeches.

We all left the cemetery silently, wanting to vent our anger. When we saw the police leaving, we roused ourselves to have a meeting, but we had overlooked the reserve agents who had stayed back. They were soon on top of us. All the women were carrying weapons. I had a hammer hidden in my raincoat and was only waiting for the men to make a move so I could use it.

"You—what do you have there?" an agent asked when he grabbed me.

"Nothing," I said.

"What do you mean, nothing? I can see something long there."

He got the hammer away from me. They also disarmed the other female comrades and put all of us in a car to take us to headquarters. We had almost reached the office

"Here on the corner's fine!" I said, to the driver, as if I were in a taxi. The agent laughed.

"Oh, Benita," he said, "why do you make more problems for yourself?" You should be home cooking beans instead of running around like this. What is all this business? Listen, if I let you go, do you promise you'll stop getting in trouble?"

"I promise."

He let us all go free.

THE FIGHT AGAINST
THE BROWN SHIRTS

We had two big fights with the Brown Shirts. The first one was in the Santo Domingo Plaza, when we were celebrating the opening of the new Party locale and the anniversary of the death of Karl Marx. The Party had organized a meeting. There were many announcements for it. Everyone was excited. Since nobody expected the Brown Shirts to show up, no one was prepared to have to confront the enemy there. They had appointed me to sell "El Machete," the central organ of the Communist Party.

The Brown Shirts showed up after the meeting had started. They charged at the Communists with heavy clubs, stones, knives, pistols and sticks. Carlos Sánchez Cárdenas, who was speaking at the time, was wounded. Many other comrades were wounded in that first clash. There was a moment of confusion because of the surprise. I realized that I had to start fighting, and I started organizing some of the comrades and people of the town who were there. The Brown Shirts were really giving it to the Communists and there were many comrades wounded; then the battle started up again. They used their pistols and knives and we used our stones and sticks. We were going to lose, of course, but we gave a good fight.

We were right in the middle of it when I noticed a comrade clubbing the Brown Shirts with a crutch. It was a Party comrade, Emilio Arias, who sold old books in the Hidalgo market. This comrade had recently joined the Party. Since we held a lot of meetings near his stall at the market, he had heard our speeches and had been persuaded that only the Communist Party defended the interests of the workers. Arias joined the Party. A few days later he became sick with typhus and they took him to the hospital; as a consequence of his illness they had to amputate both his legs, one around the knee, the other one near his ankle. Because he had his legs cut off at two different lengths, our comrade had great difficulty in walking and had to use two crutches.

I recognized Arias there in the middle of the battle. He had just been released from the hospital. The stumps of his legs were still fresh. He was very skinny; his eyes were bulging out, and he had lost all his front teeth. He looked horrible and magnificent at the same time. Every time he clubbed a Brown Shirt, he would fall down like an old bundle of clothes, since he couldn't hold himself up on his uneven legs.

He got up as best he could and hurled himself once again against the Facists. I ran toward him as soon as I recognized him. I pulled him up into my arms as if he were a child and sat him on the wall of the Santo Domingo gardens. "Comrade," I said to him, "you should stay out of this; you're crippled; leave this to us." Arias had a terrible look on his face; bulging eyes, mouth screwed up in anger, missing teeth—he looked like a skeleton. I left him sitting there and ran back to the fight. Soon I saw Arias up again, attacking the Brown Shirts with his crutches. I picked him up again in my arms; he barely weighed anything because he only had about half a body, and besides, he was very skinny. I sat him down on the wall again, but this time I took his crutches away so he wouldn't be tempted to get back into the mob.

I went back to give out some blows and I received some, too. I broke Arias' crutches during the riot. Later, in the middle of it all I forgot about my comrade and I didn't see him again. I still don't know what became of him.

I was yelling at the Brown Shirts and they were coming after me; the people around me came to my side and defended me, stopping me from being killed, but I was hit many times. I was leaving with some of the other comrades, and I started to vomit blood as we went by the Alameda. I'm sure it was from some internal injury. I don't remember when it happened. In the middle of a fight you don't even feel the blows. They took me to a doctor who gave me some injections and stopped the vomiting, but he kept me there until five o'clock in the morning, when my comrades took me home.

The second skirmish with the Brown Shirts was in the Zocalo, the central plaza of Mexico City, on November 20, 1935. The Party had decided to break up the Brown Shirts' parade any way they could. They had told us all to meet at the corner of Chapultepec and Bucareli Avenues, a corner they would be passing by. I was in union office number one, when our comrade Valentín S. Campa of the Political Bureau arrived. "You, Benita," he told me, "stay here to guard this spot and listen for the telephone. When the other comrades arrive, tell them where we're all meeting." I wasn't very happy about staying to answer telephones when my comrades would be out on the street fighting the Facists. The comrades were ready for a fight and no one even went to the office; they went directly to the meeting place. The only one who showed up was Carlos Salinas Vela. "What are you doing here all alone?" he asked me.

"Listening for the telephones and waiting for orders to call the people together."

Then some other comrades came. "What are you doing here, Benita?" they asked me.

"Guarding the place."

"What do you have to defend yourself with?"

"Nothing."

"Well, we'll leave you this pistol so if the Brown Shirts come, you can get at least one of them."

Then they left. It was late and no other comrades came, since they were all out on the street, and I became impatient. "Let's go over to Bucareli;" I said to Salinas Vela, "let's go find the action." We raced over there. At Bucareli and Chapultepec, we found a big demonstration of Brown Shirts on horses; they were all armed, with big bottles of pulque liquor hanging from their saddles. It made me want to scream, but my comrades held me back. "This isn't the right moment," they told me. We were few Communists there on the corner, so we went back to Lucerna Street, to see if there were more comrades there. No one. So, on to the Zocalo. In front of the National Palace there were about three hundred Communists, plus some peasant farmers who had come to Mexico City. They held a meeting there in front of the palace and told everyone not to let the Brown Shirts pass by. Nicolás Rodríguez, their chief, was already entering the Zocalo with his line. You could just tell there was going to be a bloody mess. "I wonder how many of us will never get up again after this one?" Salinas Vela said to me.

"Who knows, maybe no one," I answered.

"You can see we don't have enough people to fight all of them."

There were about five thousand Brown Shirts, armed and on horseback; they were very well organized. Just then, they turned around to pass in front of the National Palace. But there we were, all the Communists, waiting for them.

We threw ourselves on them with boards we had pulled down from the grandstands they had built for the parade. They opened their line to try to surround us and finish us off, but we retreated, still attacking them with the boards. The Brown Shirts' calvary were all around us when the comrades from the Taxi Union came in with their cars, which they used like tanks against the Brown Shirts' horses. The horses fell to the pavement, their legs up in the air. The cars broke the Brown offensive and separated the enemy. The battle lasted about forty minutes.

I had turned around to grab a rock, when I felt something falling down from my waist. I had forgotten about the pistol they had given me in the Union office. I raised it up to shoot, but at that moment a comrade went by and tore it out of my hands. "Give it to me!" he said. "You don't know how to shoot!"

I was standing with Gómez Lorenzo, Lola Gómez, Nacho Herrera and some other comrades in front of the National Palace. Then it occurred to me to grab a rifle from one of the palace guards and use it against the Brown Shirts. Naturally I was arrested. I promised to stay out of it and they released me. Salinas Vela fell near us, with a bullet wound in the stomach. This made me even more angry. I tried to go after the Brown Shirts' flag bearer, to get their flag away from them, but every time I got near it, bullets and sticks rained down on me.

It was a beautiful battle, but very uneven. Five thousand against five hundred. We had two dead and many wounded. But they also had wounded and their chief, Nicolás Rodríguez, was stabbed in the stomach, even though, unfortunately, it wasn't a serious injury.

A CRY AGAINST CÁRDENAS

I continued fighting for the Party with more and more fondness and confidence in the cause. The prisons only reinforced my faith in the Revolution. After all, in jail you learn many things, the least of which is to hate the capitalist system . . .

One day comrade Carlos Olaguíbel, a railroad man, invited me to a dance. I accepted. When we were there he introduced me to another comrade, who also worked on the railroad, and who was a member of the Party: he was Humberto Padilla. He invited me to have a beer, but I wasn't in the mood to drink that day, so we just sat down to talk. He was a petit-bourgeois who had recently joined the Party. He seemed to be a good comrade.

I had always wanted to meet a man like him. I felt that he was the man for me and that my road forward with him would be sincere and noble. We understood each other right away and soon I was his woman. He earned two hundred ten *pesos*, but since he had to help his mother, the salary wasn't enough. We had been living together one month when he had the opportunity to go south with a salary of five hundred *pesos* plus expenses. "Benita, I'm going to go," he said. This one's going to leave me, too, like the others, I thought. But it wasn't like that. Ten days after he left he sent me a telegram saying he adored me and that his only wish was to have me by his side and that's why he was sending me money, so I could go by airplane because he was impatient to have me with him. He sent me two hundred *pesos*.

I went by train as far as Tejeria; from there I took an airplane to Villahermosa and then to Salto de Agua, Chiapas, where he was. He gave me a wonderful welcome. He told me he adored me and that he would never leave me. He was enchanted and I was, too. I understood that finally I had found the great love I had always yearned for. We promised each other we would never part.

But I didn't forget the struggle or my Party. I wanted to continue, just like in Mexico City; I wanted to stay in contact with the workers.

The mayor of Salto de Agua became a good friend of ours. He sent us some horses so we could go out into the countryside. He would visit us and he treated us very well. It was getting close to September 15th, Independence Day. The mayor began to organize the celebration. There would be a party with various speakers. I asked the mayor if he would let me speak at the ceremony. "Why not?" he said. "With pleasure."

The news went around in no time. "The engineer's wife is going to speak on the 15th." I was very nervous because the day was approaching. At the time, some missionary teachers had come to Salto de Agua and they were asked to make decorations for the classroom where the party was going to be held. The missionaries painted a large poster with the Pope on one side and Lenin on the other. "Don't you want to go see the paintings the teachers made?" my husband asked me one day. We went. I made some comments in front of the workers. "The Pope," I told them, "represents capital, and Lenin, the proletariat."

Before leaving Mexico City I had seen a pamphlet written by Laborde. "Neither Calles nor Cárdenas," it said. I knew that the Communists in Mexico City were against the new President Cárdenas and I wanted to speak to the workers of the southeast about this. Finally the moment arrived. The ceremony began. The others spoke first. I had asked to be the last. I wanted to hear what the other ones were going to say so that I could refer to them in my speech. One of the teachers went up to the stage. He used the time to talk politics. "Comrades of Chiapas," he said, "our new President is a good one; we should raise our voices in joy to support the government of General Lázaro Cárdenas . . . " and he went on, with nothing but praise for Cárdenas.

Then it was my turn. It was exactly ten-fifteen when I went up on the platform. Everyone was anxious for me to speak. "She's Engineer Padilla's wife," the women were saying to each other. The mayor was very pleased, presiding over the event with a tri-color sash across his chest, proud to count among the numbers at the party a speaker from Mexico City, none other than the wife of the railroad engineer. Everyone was silent.

I had brought with me from Mexico City the idea that my Party was not in agreement with Cárdenas, and that is how I began my speech: "Comrades!" I said, "In the name of all the revolutionaries in the capitol, I condemn the speech made by the teacher who just took his turn to speak. In Mexico City, we are not in agreement with the new President, because he does not guarantee the rights of the workers, because he is in the service of the capitalists . . . " I had barely begun talking when the trouble started. People turned

around to look at each other. The mayor looked nervously around
the room. Some people hissed . . . but I kept speaking:

"On this day, in which we remember our Independence, when
Hidalgo and Morelos and other heroes fought to free us from
slavery to the Spanish, we must protest, because a man has risen to
power in Mexico who will be an enemy of the workers, who will
tighten the chains of imperialism here in Mexico . . . " I went on and
on, attacking Cárdenas.

In the room, the agitation grew. The wives of the rich men
were walking from one end of the room to the other, asking them
to shut me up, to get me down off the stage. The mayor didn't know
what to do; he stood there wiping the cold sweat off his forehead.
The teacher who had spoken before me was pale with anger. I kept
talking, despite their protests.

Until then, the poster the missionaries had painted with the
portrait of Lenin had been partly covered with a tablecloth, leaving
only the Pope. This had made me very angry. I looked for a chance
to refer to it and when I found one I said: "This painting represented
the proletariat because it was a portrait of Lenin, the chief of global
revolution . . . but you can't see it, because it has been covered up,
covered up just like the person who covered it." It turned out that
the person who had covered it was the mayor himself, my husband's
good friend who had always treated us so well.

The landowners and other rich snobs began to protest openly
against me, asking that I be removed from the stage. But I had the
satisfaction that not one of the workers there in the room demon-
strated against me; on the contrary, they listened attentively to me.
I continued my attacks on the new President and then the teacher
couldn't take any more. He got up from his seat. "People of
Chiapas!" he shouted, "if you still have strong blood running
through your veins, I call on you to defend our president Cárdenas!"

"That is a lie, professor," I interrupted him, "what is running
through the veins of the Chiapanecos is not blood, it is malaria. You
forgot to mention in your speech that you would contribute
something of your own to help improve their living conditions; for
example ask the government for medicine against malaria, or that
they build wells so the poor have good water instead of having to
drink from a river full of copper. This is what you should demand
of the government you defend so strongly . . . "

With this, the riot really got going. The professor tried to force me down from the stage. "The only ones who will get me down from here are the workers!" I told him.

"But señora, it is ten minutes to eleven and the mayor has to shout the cry of Independence!"

"Don't worry," I said,"we workers know how to shout,too. This stage is in good hands! I will give the cry; that is, if the workers will permit me."

Then I turned to the workers who were in the room to ask them whether they wanted me to give the cry of Independence. "Those who are in favor," I said to them, "show me by raising your hands." Nobody moved.

When he saw this, the teacher came after me, but I refused to go. Then he went to the people, asking them to pull me down. "No one will get me down from here!" I insisted. "I will shout the cry even if everyone is against it!"

The ones who were against it were the traitors, the landowners and their wives. To try to calm things down, I asked them to let me speak for just a few more minutes. I took the time to expose the teacher, who was a great pal of the railroad, where the workers were so exploited. I asked him why he didn't fight with the field workers to get their pay doubled; fight so that the law of the eight hour day was complied with; fight to raise the salaries of all workers; fight for the workers who lived far away from their workplaces to get them horses to transport them there—in short, I planted all the concrete and economic demands of the workers and managed to disarm the teacher, and also stay up on the stage.

When the hour came near to give the cry, I looked at my watch and said to the people, "We, who know what it is to be poor; we are the ones who will give the cry. The others have had their fill of shouting, but not us. Hidalgo and other heroes fought for the poor and now all of you will join me in the cry: "Comrades! Viva Mexico!"

"Vivaaa!"

"Long live the heroes of Mexican Independence!"

"Vivaaan!"

"Long live the workers who at this moment are fighting for the economic independence of Mexico!"

"Vivaaan!"

The mayor and all the others who were in charge of the ceremony had risen to their feet. They stood looking at each other.

"Well now what do we do?" they asked one another. "This woman has ruined Independence Day."

After I had cheered for the heroes of Independence, I stepped down from the stage. My husband was thrilled with my triumph. I was feeling very satisfied, too, because I thought I had made a good speech, and because I saw that the workers were on my side. They hadn't said one word against me and they clapped for me when I was finished.

(Now, as I write this, I understand that I was wrong in attacking Cárdenas, but at that time we didn't know him well and the Party was mistaken in its thinking.)

The authorities and the political bosses were furious with me. The next day they had a meeting to decide what to do. They agreed to arrest me and make me a prisoner of state. The merchants were also angry and started a boycott against me. The milkman stopped bringing me milk. When I would go to buy bread: "There isn't any more!" and on and on.

I thought things were really going to be bad for us, and then a group of peasant farmers came to see us. They had been at the party on September 15.

"Don't be afraid," they told me, "we are going to stand behind you in every way." I was very happy to see I had the peasants' sympathy. I thanked them. They didn't want to leave. They spent several days guarding the corridor of the house so no one could come to arrest us.

The commanding chief kept me under watch for a few days. Later, it was all forgotten. The merchants started dealing with me again. But the mayor never paid attention to me again. I didn't care; I was proud because I had won the confidence of the peasants. They would come see me and ask me to help them in their struggles. But I told them I wasn't prepared to lead a battle for the whole state of Chiapas. Besides, I had lost contact with the Party by then.

We were in Chiapas for about a year. Then we left for Campeche. We traveled around a few towns. I wanted to keep up with the struggle. We heard there was going to be a meeting in a small remote village. We made a special journey, but we arrived late, and the meeting was already over because they had started fighting with machetes . . .

Without any contact with the Party, I didn't know what had happened with the Cárdenas government. Finding ourselves in the town of Hol, I saw that Cárdenas had ordered the reopening of the churches and the people were celebrating the Day of the Virgin there. I saw that the people loved the President. I thought that was good . . .

TO WORK IS THE BEST THERE IS

When we returned to Mexico, my husband began saying, "What are we going to do about your child?"

"What do you mean?"

"I love you so much; I don't want anyone coming between us."

"But you think my daughter comes between us?"

"Don't be ridiculous; of course she does!"

We had discussions like this almost everyday, until I agreed to put her into a private boarding school. She stayed there two years. My husband got what he wanted. He succeeded in separating me from my daughter. Then he started trying to stop me from going to the Party, from staying in the struggle. "Let's go to a meeting," I would say.

"Why don't we go to the movies instead? There's a beautiful one playing," he would answer, and discouraged me from going to meetings.

It was May 1st and I wanted to go to the demonstration. "You stay home," he said in a teasing way; "I'll go to the demonstration in your place." And so he was always stopping me. He wouldn't let the Party comrades talk to me and since I was so well known, he couldn't tell them not to talk to me; he would just pinch me and say, "I told you I don't like other people talking to you."

"But they're from the Party!"

"I don't care. I don't want you going back to the Party anymore."

This made me suffer. I would cry, thinking that I couldn't be the same, or fight like before, alongside my comrades. Because I knew that this would prevent me from being completely happy, one day it would lead to our separation. "Humberto," I would say, "if you are a Communist you can't have these petit-bourgeois prejudices. Let me stay in the movement."

"No! Don't even think about it!"

"Who would think that a Communist could . . . "

The years went by. I distanced myself from the Party. I was afraid to lose my husband. I adored him! I would think: The truth is, he loves me and I love him, too. I have to leave the revolutionary movement to preserve the love I have been looking for all my life

. . . no, I will not destroy it now that I have found it.

"Benita, aren't you tired of being home all the time, washing floors and doing boring things like that? Wouldn't you like to work in an office somewhere? Why don't you go back to school? Housework is very difficult, and it makes people dull. Go look for a job, woman. One day I'll fail you, or we'll be separated, and then what will you do? Go back to your other life?"

I knew Humberto was right, and I went out to look for a job, as much to please him as because I knew it was the best thing for me. Everywhere I went people asked me, "Do you know shorthand?" "Can you type?" No, I didn't know anything like that. What could I do? I went to see Esther Chapa, a doctor. "Listen, Chapa," I said, "I need a job and you have to help me find one."

"But you don't know how to read or write or do anything."

"Well I don't care how you do it, but I have to work . . . and by the way, I know they're looking for people in the post office."

"But you have to know how to read and write to work in the post office . . . Well, let's go see Matilde Rodríguez Cabo."

We went to see Señora Rodríguez Cabo. She gave me a card to present to the director of the post office, who at that time was Morentín. I delivered it. They gave me a job, but they asked me the same questions.

"Can you take shorthand?"

"No."

"But you do know how to read and write?"

I said nothing.

"But how do you expect to work in the post office?"

"I saw them moving packages down below. I can do that."

They sent me to the Second Class Division to stuff bags of mail. Since I could spell a little, a few days later they sent me to distribute mail. The boss there treated us very badly. He called us lazy asses and tell us we were good for nothing. "You bunch of mules," he would say, "all you want is to make money without doing anything." So I proposed to my comrades that we write a letter demanding his dismissal. He found out about it, and the next day he gave us the worst bawling out ever.

Then he walked over to me. "Hey, are you a Communist?"

"Yes," I answered.

"So that's why you're going around agitating the employees to get on my back, and after I've been so considerate of you all. I might scold you at times for your own good; it's only so you'll learn to work."

He kept after me and after me, until I lost my patience. I couldn't take anymore and I grabbed him by the jacket and punched him so hard he flew across the room. He was in shock from the surprise. He reported me when I arrived late one day, just for revenge.

A few days later they sent me to the Santa María office to work at the stamp window. But I didn't know how to add and I made mistakes; I would give too much change back, but the public always returned the money. The boss I had there just made everything harder for me; he confused everything so I would come out short. One time he charged me forty *pesos* he said I had lost in *centavo* stamps. They moved me to another department.

On July 23, 1938, they organized a demonstration against the reactionary press of Mexico. Since I was on vacation and had free time, I went to the post office to see if I could recruit some comrades to go to the demonstration and carry the flag of the SCOP Union. Ten people agreed to go with me and we organized a group to wave the flag.

Humberto had told me not to go to the demonstration, that he would go with the railroad workers. I didn't think he would see me with all the people there. But there I was, standing proudly up front with the flag, when I see my husband, giving me a look that could kill. I gave the flag to a comrade and went over to see him. When he saw me coming, he got into a taxi and went home. He started beating me as soon as I got there; I asked him to forgive me for disobeying him. He finally calmed down a little and we went out to eat. But he was still angry. He got up suddenly from the table and left me there alone.

It was raining when I had finished eating. I was standing in the doorway of La Sevillana, waiting for it to stop, when a lottery ticket-seller went by. "Señorita, your ticket," he said. "Here's a lucky one."

"Don't bother me with that!"

He went away, but he came back a little while later. "Señorita, your ticket. Here's your ticket!"

I bought the ticket just so he would leave me alone. The next day my husband bought the newspaper, and I looked at the list. "Hey, guess what, I won the lottery," I told him.

"Man, you're right! You won two thousand five hundred *pesos*!"

It's strange, but I wasn't happy about it. "What's wrong with you?" Humberto asked me. "Aren't you happy?"

"It would be better if I hadn't won anything," I answered him, following the train of my thoughts. "Because there is a saying: When something bad happens, the good will come next, and when something good happens, get ready for the bad."

"You've become very superstitious."

"I don't know, but I feel I'm going to lose you and I wish I hadn't won the lottery."

"Look, stop this foolishness and let's go get the money and go out somewhere! Be happy! You'll see how much fun we're going to have."

"Fine, but first I want to put aside some of it for the Spanish Republicans, some for *La Voz*, some for my Party . . . and then, we'll go out and have fun!"

From then one I had the feeling that this money was going to bring something bad along with it. Six months later Humberto left me.

THE FIGHT FOR LOVE

I wouldn't leave the house without Humberto. Wherever we went we went together, always playing and joking. But sometimes, in the middle of all these jokes, he would become very serious, as if he were thinking of something. He would smooth out his suit, and even change the way he was walking. His face would look different then. "What's wrong?" I would ask him.

"No, nothing."

I knew what it was, even though he couldn't explain it clearly. When we got home I would complain to him. "I know I embarrass you," I would say.

"No, it's not that."

He would get upset when we spoke of these things. I know he was thinking about his family, about himself, his future, and my past . . . Above all, of my past, which he knew little or nothing about. He imagined things and became very serious and cold.

One of his sisters was going to get married; she was the only one who was still single. "Now your mother must be happy because everyone in your family is married," I said to Humberto.

"Yes, I'm the only one left."

"What do you mean? Don't you have me?"

He looked surprised. He saw that what he said had hurt me. He embraced me very tenderly.

Now I could see clearly what his worry was: his family, his married sisters, and he was living in sin with a woman who, who knows what she had done before going to live with him! These things made me feel that the time was coming when he would leave me. It made me very nervous. I knew he needed a woman who would help him in his work, but this didn't stop me from thinking that he would have to leave me...

One day Humberto didn't come home to eat. "Why weren't you here?" I asked him when he got home.

"Well, guess what, a girl from the railroad invited me to go eat at her house . . . and I'm still hungry. I didn't eat very well."

I felt something very ugly inside, something like fear and anger at the same time. "Oh, yeah? Why not?" I said.

"Because the food was so bad. Besides, she's a Protestant, and she kept getting up to pray and . . . well, I'm hungry!"

"So why did you go?" I asked him. "I'm telling you, if I ever find you with her I'll break her in half!"

"Don't be silly! I'm not going to leave you for any woman."

"I'm not worried. I know you won't be here forever. You're young. Besides, I can't give you a son. I'm no fool and I know a man's needs. I only ask you that when it happens, you tell me straight so I won't have to make a fool of myself. Jealousy is jealousy . . . "

"Calm down, it's not like you think."

Time went by. One day he tells me he's joined a basketball team. Good God! I said to myself; things are worse than I thought; my first husband also joined the Y and then left me a few days later. "I hate the Y!" I told him. "I hate sports!"

"Don't you know the railroad company demands it?"

"I just know you're going to leave me soon . . . you're all alike!"

"Look, don't go comparing me to anyone. You must have had men you treated you badly and that's why . . . "

"What do you know about my life!"

It was true; he didn't know anything about my life. I couldn't help seeing that Humberto started buying himself perfumes, like Varon Dandy; Manuel did the same when he was going to leave me; he would also get all dressed up. Humberto's joining the Y became very significant to me. Even the way they sat down to type was exactly the same: they would scratch their heads with one finger or tap their fingers on the table. It's easy to see when men are involved with another woman. The whole thing made me nervous and suspicious.

One night he came home and I was already in bed. "Turn off the light," he said.

"Turn it off yourself; I'm just as tired as you are."

He got angry. He gestured as if he was going to hit me. I was angry, too. "You don't scare me," I said. "Remember I used to give the police black eyes."

"Look, don't try to threaten me."

He hit me. I went after him and grabbed him by the neck. I almost strangled him. Then he got away from me. "That's it." he said. I want a separation."

"I knew you'd try to find an excuse for it."

"Why would you say that?"

"Because you must have another woman."

About two months went by. He was still living in the house. One time he came home very nervous, and in a hurry. "Pack my clothes," he told me, "I'm going on a trip." I felt that the moment had come. Men who want to leave a woman almost always invent a trip. I packed his clothes, thinking about everything. "I'll go with you to the station," I said when his clothes were ready.

"No, you don't have to."

We left together. We said goodbye at the corner. I kissed him. He didn't want me to. He walked a few steps and then took out his handkerchief and angrily wiped away the kiss I had given him. Then I knew that he was going to leave me and never come back. I ran back to the house crying. My neighbors saw me. "What's wrong, Benita?" they asked me.

"My husband left and I don't think he's coming back."

"But why not? We didn't hear any fight."

"I know, but I tell you he's not coming back."

"How do you know?"

"Because he took his typewriter with him."

The next day I told my comrades in the office. "But why do you think that?" they asked me.

"I don't know, but I'm sure he's betrayed me with a false trip. If you don't think so, you'll see."

I picked up the telephone and called his office. Someone called for him. They they told me he wasn't there, that he had left. I asked a male comrade to call him. Since it was a man calling, my husband answered. I grabbed the telephone. "What's going on?" I said. "Weren't you going on a trip?"

"Well, it's just that it was too late to go and I didn't want to bother you . . . "

"Oh you bastard! We'll see about this later!"

I went to wait for him at the station. He invited me to lunch, because he didn't want to go to the house. "Where are your clothes?"

"I left them at the railroad."

"Aren't you coming back home?"

"No...look, I didn't want to tell you . . . but I want a separation."

"I knew it! You're just like the others!"

Even though I was expecting it, I felt a very ugly sensation.

I wanted to hit him. I stayed still for a minute, not saying anything. I couldn't eat at all, thinking about the ugly trick he had played on me. I got up to go. "Wait," he said, "I'm going with you."

"Stay away from me."

He caught up with me. "Look," he told me, "I'm going to bring you the typewriter; you can have it because I know you want it more than I do." I didn't say a word. I went on alone, with a lump in my throat . . .

That same night he came to the house to put all the furniture in my name. I packed his suits calmly. "Who was the woman who took you away from me?" I asked him. "Is she intelligent? Is she beautiful?"

"That's not it," he answered. "The thing is . . . well . . . I realized I couldn't make you stop loving your daughter . . . "

"That's right!"

Now I realize that to him my daughter was the symbol of my past and he didn't like her living with us.

We argued a little more about it and then his things were ready. "Well, I'm going," he said. "I'll be looking out for you. Take this; it's fifty *pesos*."

"I don't want a thing! I have a job and I can manage alone."

"Take it," he insisted, "so you can buy clothes or something."

I have never cared about clothing. My friends would say to me: "You better dress well, because an elegant woman will take a man right out the back door." Even though he made enough money to pay for them, I never bought any dresses. I knew the reason women dress up is not to please their husbands, but so the world will admire them. Also, I understood that if I spent money on clothes, Humberto wouldn't have any to give to his mother.

He insisted that I take the fifty *pesos*. I knew they were the last he would give me. I took them and put them away.

We said goodbye.

I found out he had gone to Guadalajara. I did all I could to accept it, but I couldn't. I blamed the whole thing on the fight we had about turning off the light. "Señora," I said to his mother, "I'm going to Guadalajara."

"What are you up to, Benita?"

"I feel like seeing my husband."

"Look, you just stay home . . . because Humberto treated you very badly. He left you to go get married."

"Oh, is that so?"

I was left in a daze by the very idea of it. I suddenly didn't know what to say. I stood there thinking, trying to control myself. After the shock had passed, I said, "So he's marrying someone else, is he?"

I was furious, and at the same time relieved, thinking that it wasn't worth suffering over such a false man. "Well, time to fatten up a little, to make myself beautiful, and to go out on the town!"

The señora was sad for me, because she loved me very much. I really did dedicate myself to going out, to distracting myself; I would get drunk and eat so I would fill out a little. I went to Puebla and to Cuernavaca. I spent almost two hundred *pesos* on a single spree. I gained some weight. When Humberto left me I weighed ninety-six pounds. Then I went down to seventy-seven. When I found out he was getting married to the Protestant I started eating again. Now I weigh 118.

Humberto and I had been separated for four months and I still didn't feel like myself. I decided to look for an old friend of mine, an auditor I had met in Tulancingo, and the first man I lived with in Mexico City. I found out he was living in Querétaro. I went to look for him. I found him. Fifteen years had gone by. He didn't recognize me. "How can I help you, señora?" he said.

"Don't you remember me? I'm Benita."

"Benita Galeana! I don't believe it!"

We talked about our memories; we renewed our old friendship. He told me he wasn't happy with his woman, that he wanted to end his relationship with her and come live with me. Ever since I met him, fifteen years ago, he has been talking about divorcing his wife. "No," I said. "Look, you have children. Stay with your wife. I'm going back to Mexico City to continue with the struggle."

I told him I was writing a book about my life. "Please don't read it," I told him.

"Fine; I'll buy it to help sales, but I won't read it, I promise."

JUST LIKE OLD TIMES

Jaunuary 6, 1940 found me in the Fourth Sectional of the Communist Party. "Benita," a comrade says to me, "we have some meetings to go to tomorrow; we'll wait for you here at ten o'clock."

"But I can't, it's Sunday, and . . . "

"Sunday nothing, you just be here tomorrow."

The next day I was there. It was about ten o'clock. We went to the market at San Lucas. "Benita, you have to speak."

"But it's been five years since I've been up on a stage and I don't know how things work anymore."

"That doesn't matter; you have to speak."

"Fine; what's the meeting about?"

"Well, January 7 is the anniversary of the killing at Río Blanco."

"I'll say something, fine."

Another comrade spoke before me; she was a teacher. She did very badly. Then it was my turn. I did even worse. The people in the market paid no attention to me. We went somewhere else. On the way were were talking with some comrades who were refugees from Spain. "Damn!" they were saying, "what the Party needs is some good speakers. Now we see why things are going the way they're going, if there aren't people who know how to get the public interested, and to talk clearly about their problems." I agreed with them, but I felt sad because I couldn't speak in public with the same naturalness as I did before.

We got to the corner of Claudio Bernard Streeet. We called another meeting. It was also a disaster with very few people. The people would hear us talking and leave. I spoke again, but this time I was even worse. I would forget everything. When I felt my ideas going, I would hit my forehead with my hand, but it didn't help . . .

We came to the Hidalgo market. I said I didn't want to speak. I was ashamed to have done so badly. The Spanish comrades were disappointed with us. Then a professor from Oaxaca got up on the stage (a wooden crate). There were many people there, listening to a vender who had a doll and was talking with a loudspeaker. The teacher started to speak. No one paid attention to her. The people were fascinated by the doll, who was talking about a medicine for toothaches. Then the vender started making fun of the teacher, sabotaging her by screaming louder into the microphone so no one could hear her. When I saw what he was doing, it set off a bomb inside me. "Get down!" I yelled to the teacher. "I'm going to speak now!"

I got up on the crate and yelled with all my might: "Comrades!!" All the people turned to look at me, as if they were being pulled by one string. "In the name of the women of the Communist Party, I am here to protest against those who are responsible for the hunger in Mexico..." and I went on, mentioning all the problems that are a part of such a high cost of living, the poverty that people suffer, poverty that I know so well.

The public left the doll and came over to me. "Now we're screwed, man!" the doll said.

I kept talking to the people about the need to organize so they could fight against the monopolies. Then I talked about January 7th. "Comrades, we are now celebrating the anniversary of the killing at Río Frío . . . "

"Río Blanco!" a comrade said.

But I kept on as if nothing had happened. The public loved me. "We must continue the example of our comrades at Río Blanco," I told them, "who broke into the stores and sacked them. Are you willing to go sack the stores of the rich and take the basic necessities, instead of letting you children die of hunger?" Everyone said they were willing.

When I stepped down from the crate, people came after me to hug me. "Thank you, señorita," an old woman said, "thank you for coming and helping us poor people." Others congratulated me, repeating that they were willing to go with me to join the struggle.

I was thrilled. I felt like I was back in the old days, the high days of our underground struggle, when I would call meetings everywhere and win over the people; I felt happy like in those years when the people at the neighborhood meetings would shout: "We want the comrade with the braids!"

The comrades congratulated me. "Hell!" the Spanish comrades said. "This woman has a voice! The way she was shouting, she had the public and the doll with the microphone completely under her control! If the Party had bothered to educate this woman, maybe they would have had a Pasionaria here in Mexico . . . "

I was proud and happy to feel like the free Benita of the past, confident of my contact with the masses, more ready than ever to continue in the struggle with them to take back what was theirs.